Praise for *Simp*

"An excellent introduction from two p~~eop~~ stand and espouse the Craft of the Wise. This book blends mo~~dern~~ Wicca with its origins in the Celtic, Druidic, and traditional Witch-craft forms of lore, in a way that few others have the knowledge to do. *Simply Wicca* will take the newcomer from their very first questions to a full understanding of their chosen path and lead them into an appreciation of the ways to achieve a full understanding of the Craft of the Wise."

—Kate West, author of *The Real Witches' Craft*

"Lisa and Anton bring the gift of truly being able to take the journey through the eyes and in the footsteps of a genuine seeker of the Craft of the Wise, asking and answering the questions of a seeker in a sen-sible, practical and magickal way."

—Ashley Mortimer, Trustee of Centre for
Pagan Studies/Doreen Valiente Foundation

"Reading like a conversation with warm and wise friends, *Simply Wicca* lays out a clearly marked map for the seeker, fills their pack with tools, meditations, and rituals to move them further along the path, and serves as a trusted guide and cherished companion for the journey."

—Jhenah Telyndru, author of *Avalon Within*

simply

wicca

About the Authors

Lisa and Anton Stewart live in the historic village of New Paltz, nestled at the foot of the Shwangunk Ridge, an area of outstanding natural beauty in the Mid-Hudson Valley of New York State. It was here that they founded The Church of the Eternal Circle, New York's first federally recognized Celtic Wiccan Fellowship.

They have honored the Old Gods by offering a safe and sacred space to gather, facilitating rites and rituals, and ministering to the needs of their spiritual community for over twenty-five years.

Being both witches and accomplished musicians, they created the beautiful and profoundly moving album, *Circle in a Box*, to serve as the soundtrack for a complete Wiccan ritual.

As self-confessed Preservers of the Path, they have dedicated their lives to ensuring the survival of the Craft of the Wise through programs of education and training, and by raising witches in their Welsh-Celtic tradition of Wicca.

LISA & ANTON STEWART

simply
wicca

a Beginners Guide to
the Craft of the Wise

Llewellyn Publications
Woodbury, Minnesota

FIRST EDITION
First Printing, 2020

Book design: Samantha Penn
Cover design: Kevin Brown
Interior art by Llewellyn Art Department
Tarot card illustrations are based on those contained in *The Pictorial Key to the Tarot* by Arthur Edward Waite, published by William Rider & Son Ltd, London, 1911

Llewellyn Publications is a registered trademark of Llewellyn Worldwide Ltd.

Library of Congress Cataloging-in-Publication Data (Pending)
ISBN: 978-0-7387-6204-3

Llewellyn Publications
A Division of Llewellyn Worldwide Ltd.
2143 Wooddale Drive
Woodbury, MN 55125-2989
www.llewellyn.com

Printed in the United States of America

This book is dedicated to the Old Gods and the ancestors,
without whom we would not be.

Contents

preface

Becoming a Witch (The Journey Home)

Whether you have been a Witch for many years, or are just now stepping onto this well-worn path, we hope this book is of some service to you and the ancient ones.

Almost every time someone comes to this way of life, they liken it to a homecoming. They say such things as: "I feel as if I am remembering, and not just learning"; "I can't believe someone would think this way of life is evil or negative"; or, "I have always known I was a little different—I could hear things, sense things, and loved nature, animals, plants, and trees."

Some are content in walking their own path, with no guides other than their spiritual ones. But for others, they seek more. They want to "know" the secrets and learn the Mysteries within the setting of a group tradition. They want to become a Witch in a more defined and structured way.

Certainly, there are folks practicing Witchcraft from all walks of life—Hedge Witches, conjurers, and even some Christian

Witches. But this book is for those Witches who seek to become well versed in the Craft of the Wise—those Wiccans who aspire to follow a tradition, mapped out on a well-worn path.

They desire to reach out and touch those who have gone before them, those who are still a part of them, and those who are calling them to seek.

Accordingly, we make no apologies for the fact that this book is written from the perspective of our own, well-established tradition. We fully appreciate that traditional, old-school Wicca will not appeal to everyone, but a lot of the information included here has been gleaned over the many years we've been walking this path and some of it learned through bitter personal experience.

Our own tradition is one of Celtic Wicca that honors a Welsh/ Brythonic pantheon. It has roots in traditional Gardnerian/Alexandrian Wicca but has evolved to more fully combine the three overlapping branches of High Magic, Druidry, and Witchcraft, which were, as you'll see in chapter 1, the foundations upon which the relatively modern religion of Wicca was built. That said, in writing this book we have endeavored to make the information it contains equally applicable to all Wiccans, no matter what variety of Wicca, or particular pantheon, speaks to you.

As part of our commitment to our Craft, we have taken an oath to preserve the well-worn path on which we walk so that it remains available for those who would seek to follow—if we've done our job right—for long after we've shuffled off this mortal coil. While we cannot walk the path for you, we very much hope that at least some of the information we provide will help you avoid a few potholes, pitfalls, or wrong turns along the way.

Know this above all: To become a Witch requires work—lots of hard work, learning, practice, teaching, and dedication. Be assured that it is neither an instant process nor a quick fix to your problems.

If you have the courage to make the assay, it offers way more than mere religion—it truly becomes a way of life.

Introduction

So, you want to be a Witch...or, at the very least, you're feeling drawn to learn more about the Craft of the Wise—why else would you be holding this book in your hand?

Before we dare take the first tentative step that begins this incredible and transformative journey, we have one extremely important question for you: Why? You may wonder why we consider your motives to be so important; perhaps a brief explanation is warranted.

Over the years we have raised many Witches in our tradition, people from all walks of life and each with their own unique story to tell. Yet they all have one highly significant thing in common: they are there for the right reasons. If you are seeking to become a Witch in the belief that it will give you power over others—perhaps to bring about the return of an errant lover or exact cruel revenge upon someone who has caused you harm by way of injury, insult, or shame—then we respectfully request you put this book back on the shelf and make another selection. These are not the right reasons, and this is not the book you're looking for.

What are the right reasons? While one might be tempted to think of noble values and higher ideals that call out to the very soul of the initiate, the truth is something far humbler in origin. Simply put, something inside you has changed. It might be difficult to define precisely what it is, but things are definitely different. It's almost like you have become aware of the part of you that is aware. You are becoming conscious of the way you perceive the world around you. You are beginning to realize that things are not necessarily as they appear—that's not to say that they are otherwise … but there is certainly more to it than meets the eye.

We term this awakening an initiation. In a similar vein to initiating an explosion, it is a profound and permanent change. It is not possible to un-explode a bomb once it has been detonated, nor is it possible for you to return to blissful ignorance by un-knowing what you now know.

This initiation is merely the start of the process. For some it may well be a sudden and momentous event; for others it is a more gradual process akin to a gentle nagging or an itch you can't quite reach. Whatever form it takes, one thing is for sure: You will have questions. Lots of questions.

And thus begins your search for answers. Maddeningly, however, almost every answer you find is actually another question (or six)! You become the very epitome of the ancient Zen Buddhist saying, "That which you are seeking is causing you to seek."

It is certainly possible that this may become the source of immense frustration; just like the noble prince Pwyll's ill-judged pursuit of Rhiannon in the first branch of the Mabinogi, the elusive prize remains beyond reach, no matter how hard you try. Pwyll is so enraptured with the beautiful young maiden ambling leisurely ahead of him on horseback that he exhausts his own horse trying to catch up with her. No matter how hard he pushes his horse, he simply cannot catch up, even though her horse never does anything more than amble.

So ease up, catch your breath, and relax for a moment. It's not just you against the world; there is help at hand. There are those who have trodden this well-worn path before you; as preservers of the path, they will gladly lend a guiding hand—perchance to help you see that it's possible to try too hard.

One of the first gems of wisdom to be acquired by the initiate is not so much what to seek as where to look for it. Perhaps the mother of modern Witchcraft, Doreen Valiente, summed it up best in her beautiful Charge of the Goddess:

> … know that the seeking and yearning will avail you not unless you know the mystery—for if that which you seek, you find not within yourself, you will never find it without.[1]

It is evident that the journey of the initiate involves a voyage of self-discovery. But here's a word of warning: While this journey is undoubtedly highly rewarding if successfully completed, it can be both arduous and daunting. The Craft of the Wise is definitely not for the faint-hearted.

In fact, it's fair to say that the path to becoming a Witch is akin to a hero's journey: The road is long and hard, you will face adversity and loneliness, and your resolve will be constantly tested by the doubts that linger in the dark recesses of your mind. Yet it is a journey you must take if you are to be successful in your quest to become a Witch. More importantly, it is a journey for which there are no shortcuts. You can't simply buy this, read that, do a couple of things,

---

1. Doreen Valiente, *The Charge of the Goddess: The Poetry of Doreen Valiente* (Brighton, UK: The Doreen Valiente Foundation, 2014).

and collect your badge. You have to do the work, *and* you have to do it yourself.

Ours is a Mystery tradition. You cannot learn about the Mysteries simply by reading a book or attending a course. The Mysteries can only be experienced, not taught, and you must experience them for yourself. This is a journey you must take for yourself, even if it is fraught with difficulty and danger. You will no doubt experience highs, lows, tragedies, and triumphs along the way. But so long as you have perfect love and perfect trust in your heart, you will come to no harm. You must know that at the very core of your being the gods and goddesses, the ancient and mighty ones, your ancestors and guardian spirits, and those mortals who have sworn to guide you along the path will never ask more of you than you are truly capable. Even if you feel you cannot, you can.

Perfect love and perfect trust (especially in yourself) are your two most powerful allies that act as magickal passwords to unlock the door to the Mysteries, a door for which there is no key. So long as you keep them pure in your heart, you will, just like the hero, emerge victorious at the end of your journey.

one

What's with Wicca?

Before setting out on the path, it's probably prudent to have some idea of where the journey will take you; hence our beginning this book by taking a look at the Neopagan religion of Wicca.

We will provide a brief history along with a quick who's who of the movers and shakers within the Craft and the contributions they have made to shape it into the religion we know today.

Finally, we will consider why Wicca, with its roots planted firmly in the past, is becoming increasingly relevant in modern society.

The Craft of the Wise

As we use this term extensively throughout this book, it's probably a good idea to start by explaining exactly what it is. The Craft of the Wise, often shortened to just "the Craft," derives its title from the same Anglo-Saxon *wica*, which gave rise to the name "Wicca." *Wica*, as you'll learn later in this chapter, means "wise one" or "Witch." The word "craft" implies particular skills and knowledge, usually learned over a period of time.

Although the titles Wicca and the Craft of the Wise are largely interchangeable, we do have a strong affinity for the latter, as it subtly conveys the need for dedication and study to gain the skills and knowledge required to effectively practice your craft.

What Exactly Is Wicca?

Wicca, per se, is defined as a Neopagan religion, although some would say that it is far more than a mere religion and to describe it as such actually denigrates the Craft.

Nonetheless, there can be no denying the fact that Wicca has become officially recognized as a religion by governments the world over. Depending upon your viewpoint, that designation might be for better or for worse, but it does at least offer some degree of protection from religious discrimination under the law, or at least in theory—your mileage may vary. Unfortunately, being legally entitled to practice your religion is no guarantee that you will not be subject to discrimination. Sometimes it's best to apply the wisdom contained within the Witches' pyramid (to know, to will, to dare, and to keep silent) and know when to keep your mouth shut and your personal beliefs just that—personal.

Now that we've established that Wicca can be properly described as a Neopagan religion, we come to what makes Wicca what it is and how it differs from other Pagan religions.

It certainly would not be an unreasonable observation to say that there are a great many different flavors of Wicca, but rather than getting bogged down in the mind-boggling array of differences, let's try to focus on the similarities.

There are many variants in other religions too. Within Christianity are Catholics, Methodists, Lutherans, Anglicans, Protestants, Baptists, Evangelists, Mormons, Jehovah's Witnesses, Seventh Day Adventists, and many, many more. One could probably write a book about the differences between these faiths, but all have one thing in common—a belief in Christ.

So, what's the common thread running through Wicca? What are its similarities? While there will always be exceptions, it would be reasonably accurate to describe Wicca as an Earth-based, polytheistic, Neopagan religion. There are some words here that warrant further explanation. We've already discussed religion, but what of Neopaganism? The prefix "neo-" comes from the Greek *neos*, meaning "new." Hence, Neopagan could be interpreted as a new or revised form of Paganism.

We are then brought to the word "Pagan." It should be made clear that the terms "Pagan" and "Wiccan" do not mean the same thing. Certainly, all Wiccans are Pagan, but not all Pagans are Wiccan. The word *pagan* was originally a Latin term Romans used during early Christianity as a derogatory term for people who lived outside the cities, country dwellers who knew naught of civilization and the then-fashionable and new religion. Similarly, the term *heathen* also originally referred to folks who dwelled on the heath, although this word is now more commonly used to describe followers of Nordic Neopagan or reconstructionist traditions, such as Asatru.

Despite its original usage, the Roman slur seems to have stuck; for a great many followers of the revealed religions, the term "Pagan" has since come to refer to almost any spiritual belief or practice outside of the scope of the mainstream Abrahamic religions of Judaism, Christianity, and Islam. However, this usage is a gross oversimplification, as there are more than five thousand religions and/or spiritual practices in the world today, very few of which would identify as Pagan.

"Polytheistic" and "polytheism" simply refer to the practice of honoring many gods, although traditional Wicca could equally be viewed as being duotheistic, insomuch as it honors both the God and the Goddess. That said, there are forms of Wicca, such as Dianic Wicca, that honor only the Goddess, but that's not what we'll cover here.

Within traditional Wicca, the God represents the Divine Masculine and is typically represented by the sun, whereas the Goddess represents the Divine Feminine and is represented by the moon and/ or Mother Earth. Rather than an overarching and somewhat vague description (e.g., "the Divine"), it is typically common for Wiccans to honor specific deities within their rites and rituals, particularly in a group setting. Repeatedly working with the same deities can be of great benefit in building a closer working relationship. Though it's covered more deeply in chapter 7, in our tradition, we honor Cerridwen and Cernunnos.

It's also worth mentioning something that continues to remain a source of debate amongst Wiccans—namely whether the deities are gods and goddess in their own right (true polytheism), or are actually aspects of a single god, goddess, or divine essence (henotheism). Don't worry, we're not going to ask you to take sides. As far as we're concerned, this is a matter for your personal conscience and has no bearing on your ability to form a close working relationship with your chosen deities.

Having covered the polytheistic, Neopagan religion part of the description, we now come to the "earth-based" bit. In essence, this is what truly makes Wicca what it is. As we've discussed, there are many other polytheistic Pagan religions that differ widely from Wicca. As you progress along this path, you'll also come to realize that there are also many forms of Wicca that differ substantially from each other. The common thread that ties them all together is the natural rhythms or cycles of the earth, more specifically the movement of the sun and moon in relation to the earth.

We now know from scientific observation that the earth is a spherical planet that orbits around the sun at the center of our solar system, not a flat patch of ground where the sun rises in one part of the sky and sets in another, as our ancient predecessors once believed. Incidentally, the geocentric (Earth-based) model was the official position of the Catholic Church right up until 1992, when Pope John Paul II officially accepted the findings of Galileo and granted him pardon for the crime of heresy. Galileo had deduced that Earth was not the center of the universe, as the church claimed, but was a planet moving around the sun, something he was forced to recant under threat of torture before the Inquisition in 1633.

Nonetheless, we see from where we're standing, so it makes sense to look at this movement from a geocentric viewpoint. Accordingly, Wicca honors the never-ending dance of sun and moon in constant chase across the sky, the ceaseless ebb and flow of longer days and shorter nights, manifest in the endless cycle of the seasons. This Wheel of the Year, as it is known, is celebrated at sabbats, special ceremonies marking key points throughout the year. The cycles of the moon are celebrated at esbats, ceremonies honoring a particular phase of the moon in relation to the Wheel of the Year. Although some traditions may honor only the sabbats (and even that number may vary, as some Wiccan traditions only celebrate the four major ones), this practice is the common thread running through Wicca.

Before we dive into the history of Wicca, it's important that we address the subject of Witchcraft. It's fair to say that even today, the word "Witch" still strikes fear into the hearts of a good many people. Ever since the Late Medieval period when the church officially recognized the existence of Witches and granted full papal approval for the establishment of an inquisition to seek out and eliminate their kind, Witches have been the subject of relentless fear-mongering, culminating in a widespread moral panic that spawned the Witch trials of the sixteenth to eighteenth centuries. Even though the mass hysteria of the "burning times" has long since passed, Witches and Witchcraft are still perennial favorites for the writers of horror films to this very day. We apologize if you're one those people for whom the word "Witch" triggers a deep-seated anxiety, but there really is no way to sugarcoat this: Wicca *is* modern Witchcraft.

In common with the theme that all Wiccans are Pagan, in our mind, and certainly within our tradition, all Wiccans *are* Witches. On the other hand, however, not all Witches are Wiccan. It is certainly possible for someone to practice folk magic or Witchcraft without Wicca's religious or spiritual component. But as you progress through this book, you will see for yourself that it is impossible to follow the path of Wicca without practicing magic. Even if you never cast a spell in your life, the very rites and rituals that form the Craft of the Wise are acts of natural and sympathetic magic in and of themselves. That said, we've both met more than one person who claimed to be Wiccan but definitely not a Witch. We can only assume the word "witch" has such negative connotations for them that denial is the only viable option.

The History of the Craft

Although it draws upon innate wisdom and knowledge perhaps as old as time itself, it may surprise you to learn that the Wiccan religion we know today is actually quite modern.

There is much debate about who originally coined the term "Wicca," but there can be no doubt as to who brought it to the attention of the world in the latter half of the twentieth century—an oddly eccentric and rather well-to-do Englishman by the name of

Gerald Brosseau Gardner (1884–1964). It's fair to say that virtually every Wiccan tradition in existence today has its roots in Gardnerian Wicca. For this reason, Gerald Gardner has come to be known as the father of modern Witchcraft. Gardner was born to wealthy parents who had a business in the timber trade. The firm, which specialized in the import of exotic hardwoods, had been founded by his father's great-great-grandfather, Edmund Gardner, a fellow who had managed to successfully climb the social ladder to the point where he was awarded the rare honor of becoming a "Freeman of the City of Liverpool," a title that in the context of the mid-eighteenth century was a rare honor indeed. It recognized that he had escaped the drudgery of serfdom and elevated himself to become a respected member of the landed gentry. Suffice it to say, Gerald Gardner was the epitome of old money.

That's not to say Gerald's childhood was a particularly easy one, for he was quite sickly and suffered from bouts of acute asthma, a condition seriously exacerbated by the polluted atmosphere of the heavily industrial Lancashire in which he lived. The dense winter smog was especially hard for him. In common with wealthy, upper-middle-class children of the day, Gardner was largely raised by his nanny rather than his parents. In Gerald's case, she was a young Irishwoman by the name of Josephine McCombie, whom he affectionally called Com.

Although there is much conjecture surrounding her true motives, Com offered to take the child to warmer climes in order to ease his suffering, albeit at his father's expense. So, travel they did—so extensively that Gerald never actually received a formal education nor attended school. But being a determined sort, he taught himself to read and write. And did he ever love to read! One of his favorite and most influential books was *There Is No Death* by Florence Marryat, a book that propounded the immortality of the soul; he found the subject matter captivating.

Around the turn of the twentieth century, Com met her soulmate, David Elkington, in Ceylon (now Sri Lanka) and decided to marry him. Elkington ran a highly successful tea plantation, so it was agreed that the young Gerald should continue to reside with the newly married couple and learn the tea trade.

Com and her new husband, David, set up home in Kandy, a city that, aside from being one of the most spiritually revered places within the Buddhist faith, was also literally right next door to the famous (or, depending upon your viewpoint, notorious) Aleister Crowley. Their being neighbors was something that would prove to be highly significant in the coming years.

Most all of us who come to this path can, upon reflection, identify the one pivotal point where we begin to question all that we've been taught in our formative years and perhaps even begin to reject our conditioning. In Gerald Gardner's case, it was at this exact point in his story where we believe he encountered his personal tipping point and began to reevaluate the core tenets of his beliefs.

For the sake of expediency, we'll largely gloss over Gardner's working life and fast-forward to his retirement, when things really got busy. Suffice to say that he moved in the right circles, rubbed shoulders with some interesting people, and gained a strong interest in folklore, history, archaeology, anthropology, and Spiritualism.

On her husband's retirement from the civil service in Malaya, Gerald's wife, Donna, persuaded him to return to England, where they eventually settled in the village of Highcliffe, Hampshire on the southern fringe of the New Forest. Gardner quickly found that the colder climate really didn't suit him, and he soon started to develop issues with his health. His doctor suggested he try nudism, and although

Gerald was initially skeptical, he found that it really did cure what ailed him, and quickly became a strong proponent for the practice.

It was also in Highcliffe that Gerald had a brief flirtation with Rosicrucianism but quickly became disenchanted with the group's leader. Nonetheless, he struck up a strong friendship with a few members of the group who kept to themselves for the most part. He soon learned that these were members of the New Forest Coven and believed them to be one of the last surviving covens of an ancient Witch-cult that pre-dated Christianity. It's probably worth pointing out that at the time (1939), Witchcraft was still illegal in Britain under the Witchcraft Act of 1735. Accordingly, the members of the coven very much kept themselves to themselves out of necessity.

Eventually, Gardner won their trust and, on one fateful night in September of 1939, was taken by the coven to the home of "Old Dorothy" Clutterbuck, where he was stripped naked and led through an initiation ritual into the Craft. It was partway through this ritual that he heard the term *Wica*, which he recognized from his studies as an Old English word to mean "Witch." Gardner himself did not use the term "Wicca" to refer to the practice of the New Forest Coven or even the group he subsequently founded, but it's at the point of his initiation where this word starts to take on a special significance.

Following his initiation, Gerald continued to explore other avenues of spirituality. Naturism remained an important practice for him, and he regularly attended a nudist colony near Bricket Wood in Hertfordshire. It was here he met and became close friends with Ross Nichols. Gardner had become fascinated with Druidry, having recently joined the Ancient Druid Order, and introduced Ross to the religion. This meeting would prove to be highly significant, as Ross Nichols became enraptured with Druidry and went on to become Chairman of the Ancient Druid Order before branching out to found the Order of Bards, Ovates and Druids (OBOD).

At the end of World War II, Gardner and his wife decided to up sticks from Hampshire and move to Bricket Wood. Gerald had purchased the former Four Acres naturist club, of which he used to be a member, along with an adjoining plot of land he renamed "Five Acres." He also acquired a sixteenth-century Witches' cottage he had arranged to be dismantled, shipped to, and reassembled on the site.

Fearing that the "Old Religion," as he termed it, might die out, he formed his own coven to meet at the Witches' cottage in Bricket Wood, from where he eagerly started to seek out new members.

It was about this time when he reconnected with an old friend he'd met before the war, Arnold Crowther, a performing magician who worked magic with a "c" (as in pulling a rabbit from a hat), as opposed to High Magick with a "k," meaning ceremonial magick. Despite Crowther's stage magic, he did also have some serious connections within High Magick as well.

Crowther introduced Gardner to a friend of his, the occultist Aleister Crowley, the very same person to whom he'd quite literally lived next door to while residing at his adolescent home in Kandy.

Recognizing Crowley's wealth of esoteric knowledge and wishing to glean as much he could from this venerable high magician, he quickly struck up a friendship.

For his part, Crowley believed that Gardner might be able to help revive the ailing British branch of the Ordo Templi Orientis (O.T.O.), of which Crowley was the head. Accordingly, he raised Gerald to the fourth degree within the order and passed on a veritable trove of information describing their rites and rituals.

There was some talk of Gardner becoming head of the British branch of the O.T.O., but for a number of reasons, this did not come to pass. However, Crowley's material did not go to waste; it became, according to those who knew, the basis of Gardner's first Book of Shadows, *Ye Bok of Ye Art Magical*.

As Gardner's wife, Donna, had no interest in Witchcraft, he persuaded Edith Woodford-Grimes, the member of the New Forest Coven into which Gardner had been initiated, to become the High Priestess of his new Bricket Wood Coven.

Incidentally, the Bricket Wood Coven, the very first in the Gardnerian line, being centered in 1946, still exists and is active to this very day, although they no longer meet in the Witches' cottage.

Before long, Gerald and Edith, whom he referred to by her magickal name, Dafo, had begun to initiate others into the Craft. Nonetheless, Gardner was still deeply concerned that the Craft was in perilous decline and redoubled his efforts to ensure its survival. Given that Witchcraft was still illegal, he found himself in somewhat of a quandary on how best to do this.

Eventually he devised a plan to publicize the Craft by writing a book called *High Magic's Aid*, under the pen name of Scire, which was published by The Atlantis Bookshop in London. While ostensibly a work of fiction set in the twelfth century, the book details actual magickal workings.

In 1951 the archaic Witchcraft Act of 1735 was repealed by Parliament and it was no longer against the law to be a Witch. So, Gardner started to actively court the press in an attempt to bring renewed vigor to the "Old Religion" by generating interest in the Craft. Unfortunately, this move was met with disdain bordering on hostility by some members of the New Forest Coven, who still very much wanted to keep to themselves. Nonetheless, it did bring Wicca to the attention of a woman by the name of Doreen Valiente, who'd recently attained the ripe old age of thirty, having just endured her first Saturn return. The planet of restriction and karmic lessons, Saturn takes about 29.5 years to make a complete cycle of your natal chart, an event called a Saturn return. This event marks the point where we reap what we've sown and may result in some difficult life lessons. Even the glyph, ♄, looks like a chair—sit down, because you're going to learn something!

Valiente had developed a deep interest in the occult following the end of World War II and was familiar with the work of historian, anthropologist, and folklorist Margaret Murry, who had put forward the theory of the existence of a pre-Christian Witch-cult she termed "the Old Religion." On learning that there may still be pockets of this surviving to that very day, Doreen's interest was certainly piqued. She wrote to Gerald, and they began a correspondence that would last for several months before Gardner agreed to meet with her.

The meeting was to take place at the home of Edith Woodford-Grimes (Dafo), in Hampshire. And, in the summer of 1953, Doreen Valiente was initiated into the coven by Gerald Gardner. Valiente rose quickly through the ranks to become High Priestess, eventually replacing Dafo (Woodford-Grimes), who had become increasingly frustrated by Gardner's constant publicity-seeking.

Doreen's initiation into Wicca was to be a truly pivotal event, for her contribution to the Craft is of immense importance. While Gerald Gardner has been called the father of modern Witchcraft, Doreen Valiente has come to be known as its mother. Valiente had an uncanny gift for poetry. Recognizing the obvious Crowley influence upon Gardner's Book of Shadows, *Ye Bok of Ye Art Magical*, she took it upon herself to almost completely rewrite it. She replaced much of the arcane and somewhat stuffy language focused on the "ceremonial magic" component, with beautiful and evocative poems that drew more upon the emotional aspect of the Craft as well as the nature of nature itself.

Some say that Valiente brought a woman's touch to the previously largely misogynistic realm of High Magick to create the unique blend of masculine and feminine qualities that form the Wicca we know today. Certainly, the rites and rituals within our own tradition would not be so emotionally engaging and deeply moving, were it not for her. One of her best-known pieces is the Charge of the Goddess, a work that is both profoundly moving and deeply magickal.

> There shall ye assemble, ye who are fain to learn all sorcery, yet have not yet won its deepest secrets: to these will I teach things that are yet unknown.[2]

This poem is used by Wiccan groups the world over. In fact, we ourselves often read the Charge of the Goddess as part of our own rites and rituals. We've included the entire poem (by kind permission of the Doreen Valiente Foundation) in chapter 8.

Although this and other pieces of her work—such as "The Witches' Chant" (also known as Witches' Rune) and "The Witches' Creed" (also known as the Wiccan Rede)—have become cornerstones of the Craft, sadly her name is not so widely recognized, at least as yet. While Gerald Gardner is credited as being the founding father of Wicca, we would respectfully suggest that without the contributions of this incredible woman, Wicca simply would not be where it is today.

Why Do We Call It "Wicca?"

It's worth taking a look at the etymology of the word "Witch" at this point. As far as we can tell, it came into common usage in the Early Middle Ages (circa 500 CE) when one of the predominant languages of Britain was Anglo-Saxon or Old English. It's quite likely the word existed prior to this point, but we're wandering into the annals of pre-history and records are decidedly sketchy.

---

2. Valiente, *Charge of the Goddess*.

At this time the English language had gender and so there were two words: the masculine, *Wicca* (pronounced *wit-cha*), and the feminine, Wicce (pronounced *witch*).

It's commonly thought that the word equates to "sorcerer" from the Old French, *sorcier*, itself from the Medieval Latin, *sortiarius*, meaning "one who sorts or influences the fates and fortunes." However, given that Medieval Latin had very little influence over the Old English of the Anglo-Saxons, we think it's worth digging a little deeper.

Consider, if you will, wicker, as in wickerwork, where a knowledgeable and skilled craftsman bends and weaves simple wooden twigs together to create a functional object such as a basket or chair. The word "wicker" has exactly the same Old English root. Hence, we tend to think that the word Wicca is more appropriately translated as: "One who influences fate and fortune by bending, shaping, and weaving the very fabric of reality." To achieve this aim requires not just knowledge, but the wisdom of how that knowledge is applied. Wicca truly is the Craft of the Wise.

Summary

In this chapter, we have given you a brief insight into the nature of Wicca and origins of this natural, Neopagan religion. We have introduced you to just a few of the people who helped the Craft of the Wise become what it is today.

You have learned that, although drawing upon ancient wisdom, Wicca itself only really came into being in the latter half of the twentieth century.

Nonetheless, the Craft of the Wise encompasses, honors, and celebrates the very nature of nature itself. To dedicate oneself to walk upon this well-worn path is to commit to following in the footsteps of those who trod before us, accepting responsibility for our own actions, and learning respect for our Mother Earth and all living things, including those on the path behind us.

This is not a journey for the fainthearted. There will no doubt be times where you question yourself and doubt it's even worth the effort.

For our part, we can only say that it's all about the journey, not the destination, and this is the most incredible journey you will ever take.

The road may be hard at times, but those ahead of you on the path will always reach back and lend a hand to help you over the hardscrabble.

two

You See from
Where You're Standing

When folks first come to this path, it's common to see the desire to progress along it as quickly as possible. However, as we've said before, it's not the destination that's important, but rather, the journey itself. The path of the Craft of the Wise is not a laser-straight line that can be negotiated at light speed; it has many twists and turns, and quite a few ups and downs along the way. Within this chapter we hope to show you that even these are a necessary part of awakening to the magick and that there are no shortcuts. Only by personally experiencing the Mysteries will you be able to deepen your understanding and broaden your perspective. But before you can experience the Mysteries, you must be properly prepared and ready to experience them. Please understand that time spent in preparation is never time wasted. You wouldn't want to set out to climb Snowdon on a whim, wearing only a T-shirt and sneakers.

It's All About the Journey

Your journey, to be precise. Every Witch's journey is unique to them; as much as this is a journey along a well-worn path, it is equally an expedition into the uncharted territory of the innermost reaches of the psyche. Journeys of self-discovery are, by their very nature, unsettling. Sometimes what lies beneath may be deeply troubling and open old wounds, but it's only by doing so that the necrotic tissue can be excised, allowing complete healing to take place.

We humans are fragile and complex creatures. We are capable of the most beautiful, generous, caring, and selfless acts of love, and equally capable of the most depraved acts of hate, violence, and cruelty. The potential for all of these lies within each and every one of us, which is why journeying within can sometimes be decidedly scary. Perhaps you remember the scene from *Star Wars* where Luke receives instruction from his Jedi Master, Yoda, who tells him to enter an ominous-looking cave.

"I'm not frightened," declares Luke.

"Oh, you will be … you will be!" asserts Yoda, in a particularly sinister manner.

"Wh-why? Wh-what's in there?" asks Luke.

Yoda responds: "Only what you take with you."

To further paraphrase Yoda's wisdom, if a Witch you'll be, then journey you must. You have to find your place of peace and power and become comfortable not merely within your own skin, but within your own psyche as well. One of the most significant Mysteries is that in order to truly see inside yourself, you have to look from the outside.

We've said it before and will say it many times again: you see from where you're standing. When it comes to objective introspection, you're likely to find your view somewhat occluded if you're standing in your own way. Consider the following analogy:

We're standing in a beautiful forest. "Look at this magnificent forest. Isn't it just amazing?" we say. "What forest?" you reply. "All I can see is this huge tree right in front of me. Maybe if I take a chain saw and cut it down, I'll be able to see the forest."

This approach is definitely not going to help you. May the gods forbid such foolishness, but if you were to cut down the tree, you would still find your view obstructed by other trees. Should you continue to cut down trees, eventually your view will be unimpeded, but there will no longer be a forest to see.

You must change your perspective by actually moving to a place where you can see the forest from a distance. For only by detaching yourself from the situation that seeks to occupy the entirety of your attention can you truly make an objective assessment of what you're actually dealing with.

Having learned to recognize the magnificence and splendor of the forest from afar, you will be able to re-enter the woodland and truly experience its beauty from within, your new appreciation of the forest being aided by a deeper understanding of its nature, gained from seeing it as a whole. It will no longer be a bunch of trees that obscure your view, but rather a colony of sentient beings who are aware of your presence within.[3] Don't be surprised if they actually start talking to you!

The same is true of yourself. You must learn to recognize the traits that hamper your progress on the path, something more readily achieved from an external perspective. As is often said, "If only we could see ourselves as others see us." While this may be somewhat

3. Peter Wohlleben, *The Hidden Life of Trees: What They Feel, How They Communicate—Discoveries from a Secret World* (Melbourne, AU: Black Inc., 2016).

helpful, it is not the perfect solution; things may not always be as they appear at first sight, and a purely external perspective lacks context. One cannot fully appreciate the true nature of the forest until they have actually walked into the wood and experienced it from the inside. You need to acquire the skills necessary to be able to make an objective assessment of yourself, *and*—and this is absolutely key—to make this assessment without judgment. For most folks, this means radically changing the way we look at things, especially ourselves. We need to re-think our thinking, a process that begins with serene acceptance. We must accept that our traits are neither good nor bad; they are simply traits. We must consciously choose not to struggle against ourselves, as internal conflict is a battle that cannot be won.

All too often we find fault with ourselves and fight to repress, ignore, or otherwise subdue these undesirable traits, but this is almost always an exercise in futility. If you have an injured knee and need to run a race, hacking your leg off is not going to help you run faster.

Perhaps the most important thing in learning to look at things in a completely different way, is actually learning to look. To paraphrase Sherlock Holmes, most of us see but we do not observe.

Within our tradition, a very important part of the training and work of an initiate is focused upon developing the acuity of the senses. One of the ways we've found to be most effective at getting folks to observe rather than just see is to have them focus on a particular color and make mental note whenever they encounter it. At the end of the day, we ask that they recount their experiences: When and where did they see the color? What were the circumstances? What feelings did it invoke? What else did they notice, and so on?

We strongly recommend that every aspiring Witch should keep a special book where you write down notable thoughts, dreams, feelings, events, happenings, or other general oddities. In our tradition, we call this book a "weirdness journal."

In modern society, we humans have become increasingly distanced from nature. We live, work, and travel in comfortable, heated or air-conditioned environments unaffected by the changing of the seasons. Artificial light has transformed the length of our days, so that they are no longer constrained by the rising and setting of the sun. Even our imagination has suffered under a relentless onslaught of television, computer games, virtual reality, and social media, all of which constantly strive for our attention. Our isolation from the natural world is almost complete.

In order to awaken to the magick, one has first to awaken the senses. And there is no better way to do this than reconnecting to nature.

Go take a look at a tree. But don't just look, *observe*. Look closely at the bark on its trunk. Study the lands, cracks, and grooves of its surface. Contemplate the patterns they make. What do they make you think of, and how do they make you feel?

You should repeat this process and revisit the tree at different times of the year. Notice how it changes with the seasons. If you can, go back to the tree exactly one year after you first met. Look closely at what's different and what's stayed the same. We bet you'll notice things you didn't see last year.

Repeat this process as often as you can with almost everything you encounter until it almost becomes a habit. Gradually you will start to awaken your senses and see the things that have been hidden in plain sight. Remain mindful that this is a process, and processes take time. Exactly how much time is impossible to say, as it varies widely between individuals. However, there is one thing we can say with certainty—there are no shortcuts and impatience will only impede your progress.

The harder you push against the door that has no key, the stronger it will resist you. It is not possible to force your way through the door that leads to the Mysteries; you simply have to allow it to open.

Perhaps one of the most effective remedies to impatience (aside from serene acceptance) is to have realistic expectations. As we said before: "One cannot learn the Mysteries, for they cannot be taught—they may only be experienced." And experience itself may only be gained over time. This is, after all, the Craft of the Wise; wisdom is not attained without knowledge gained from experience.

When it comes to knowledge, there are things we know, and there are things we know we don't yet know. But it's wisdom that allows us to understand there are many, many more things we don't even know we don't know.

We humans think we're really smart; heck, we can split the atom, build supercomputers, and send rockets into space. But seldom do we accept that there are things we simply don't know we don't know; instead, we attempt to make things fit the constructs of our understanding rather than allowing our understanding to be broadened.

You might as well get used to the idea that Get Witch Quick schemes don't work. If you were just handed everything and didn't have to work for it, you most probably would not respect it and you most certainly would have been robbed of all the ah-ha moments that go along with uncovering, discovering, and reclaiming your place on this well-worn path.

We mentioned at the start of this chapter the path is not a straight one. If anything, it's more of a circle than a line between two points. Certainly, it's cyclical, for it follows the Wheel of the Year, but it would be more accurate to describe it as a spiral.

When it comes to learning, repetition is key. The more times we do something, the more familiar it becomes. Everyone has the potential to learn, regardless of ability. It all comes down to desire, dedication, and commitment.

Assuming they had the desire, absolutely anyone could learn to play the piano.

Imagine, if you will, the piano teacher coming to your home and telling you to press middle C. On the first day, you have no idea what middle C even looks like, and then you find out the note actually looks like the lowercase letter b. The piano teacher tells you that your homework is to press middle C every day and listen to what it sounds like. By the second day, you already know exactly what key to press. Maybe by the third or fourth day you can even hear the tone of middle C in your head before you even enter the room where the piano resides. The more you practice, the better you will become.

The same is true of the path. When you first set off, things are decidedly unfamiliar, somewhat bewildering, and sometimes even downright strange. But each turn of the Wheel is an upward spiral where you can look back at where you were previously and apply the knowledge gained over the subsequent turns. You see from where you're standing.

Summary

In this chapter we've explained that the path of the Craft of the Wise is a Mystery tradition. You don't know what you don't know, and we can't tell you—you have to experience the Mysteries for yourself in order to truly understand them.

We've also told you that it takes time to gain experience and that you need to be patient, particularly with yourself. Impatience leads to frustration, which causes people to give up. We've had people who were learning get frustrated with us and quit, saying, "Can't you just tell us everything?" So again, try looking at it like learning to play the piano; you'll never be able do a command performance if you don't know where middle C is.

But don't ever doubt that you have the potential to learn and, in time, become adept in your Craft. Repetition is key, for the more you do something, the better at it you become. The renowned virtuoso violinist, Pablo de Sarasate, said, "For thirty-seven years I've practiced fourteen hours a day, and now they call me a genius!" In short, ability comes from desire, dedication, and commitment.

Just have an open mind, cut yourself some slack, and be patient— you see from where you're standing.

three

Elementary, My Dear Witchling!

In this section, we go over the elements, the very building blocks of both the physical and magickal worlds. We will look at the quarters, also known as the four directions, which combine to form a magickal circle. We explore the Watchtowers, the portals to the magickal realms, and the Guardians who watch over them. We discuss the elemental kings and how to build a working relationship with them. And finally, we introduce you to the art of astral journeying as we explore the elemental kingdoms.

The Elements

In the Craft, almost everything seems to come down to the elements, although the number does vary. For the Druids it's just three: land, sea, and sky. Fire is thought of as otherworldly. In High Magick, there are five elements: earth, water, air, fire, and spirit. In our tradition of Wicca, we have four: air, fire, water, and earth.

We mentioned that the elements are the building blocks of reality, physical or otherwise. You can reduce almost everything into these four attributes or qualities.

In the physical world, one could consider the elements to be the states of matter: earth is solid—matter in its most dense state. If we apply energy and heat it up, the solid will melt and become a liquid—which corresponds with the element of water. If we apply more energy, the liquid boils and becomes a gas, which corresponds with the element of air. And if we apply even more energy, the gas becomes an incandescent plasma, which corresponds to the element of fire.

As you'll learn in chapter 8, one important part of casting a circle to create a safe and sacred space between the worlds, in which to hold ritual and work magick, is invoking the elements and the elemental energies they offer. This process is often termed "calling the quarters."

Although there are groups and traditions that differ, the elements are, when casting a circle, most commonly invoked in the order of air, fire, water, and earth. This corresponds with the four directions, starting in the east and working deosil (clockwise) around the circle. This is the order in which we will discuss each of the elements and their associations.

As we call the quarters and invoke each of the directions, we can sense different energies, a different elemental being, a Guardian, color, intention, and so on.

Element	Direction	Color	Symbol	Quality
Air	East	Yellow	△	Passive Masculine
Fire	South	Red	△	Fixed Masculine
Water	West	Blue	▽	Passive Feminine
Earth	North	Green	▽	Fixed Feminine

Although the symbols might seem a little confusing at first, an easy way to remember them is that fire burns upward (the upward-pointing triangle) until it reaches the air (upward triangle with the line). Water flows downward (the downward-pointing triangle) until it reaches the earth (the line in the downward triangle).

If you are more of a visual-memory person, you could also see that air's triangle makes an A and, loosely, the earth triangle makes an E.

As you progress in your studies, you will come to realize that symbolism is important. Learning these correspondences will lend power and energy to the work you are doing. For example, if you know that you are working to call in the energies of air and you are facing east, you are looking in the right place—you are focused on the direction from which the energy will emanate and you are ready to greet it rather than having it pop up behind you and take you by surprise.

All colors have an energetic frequency, or vibration, within the electromagnetic spectrum. By envisioning the color yellow, you are sending out a universally (in the literal sense) understood vibration to welcome the energies of air. And by seeing the symbol, the upward triangle with the line, you are saying you speak their language.

But what about the elemental qualities, and what do we mean by fixed or passive? North/earth and fire/south are considered fixed energy, true or pure. In astrology, fixed means stable, determined, and persistent. In other words, inflexible, unwavering, and permanent.

Earth is the true or pure energy of the feminine, without question and unchangeable. Fire is then the balance to this, the true energy of the masculine. Again, without question and unchangeable.

Air/east and water/west are considered passive or yielding. In astrology, this energy is associated with adaptability, flexibility, and sympathy. This is the energy of the mediator, allowing for diplomacy and assisting others through transitions. Sometimes it is seen as dual in energy, having both masculine and feminine qualities.

There's a whole chapter of this book devoted to the art of circle casting, where in addition to actual physical "how-to" information, we go into greater detail about the importance of symbolism and provide some practical exercises to deepen your understanding. For now, it's worth noting the following:

Air energy is very light and lives close to the world of other. Air breathes life into fire. It is something we know is there, yet unless it combines with another element (such as fire and water creating mist), we cannot see it. We have proof of its existence; we inhale and exhale it, and without it we could not live or think properly. It governs the unpredictable, thoughts, inspiration, and positive energy. It is the place where wishes manifest and astral travel is commonplace. It introduces earth to fire, as it takes its place between them. It is passive masculine.

Fire is a vibrant energy like no other. Again, it cannot exist on its own; it needs air and fuel. Its energy is driven, passionate, and connected to the sun, the father of all life. As fixed masculine, it governs action and movement. In alchemy, it is considered the topmost of the elements. It can quickly get out of control if left on its own without instruction. It can be seen as destructive but can also clear a way forward.

Water is linked to the Mysteries, magick itself, and the moon. While it is dense, is it still fluid. Though we consider water to be passive and malleable, it can wear a hole right through a stone. It governs change, transformations, and psychism. It is enduring and knowing. We can draw much emotion and intuition from this element. And as the passive feminine, it introduces fire to earth in the circle of elements.

Earth the heaviest and densest of the elements. It is the bringer of reality, stability, protection, and growth. Think mother, seed grower, and strong roots. As said earlier, nothing would be able to grow without water and solar energy. Earth is the womb, the creatrix, the solidifier. It is the fixed feminine.

The energetic qualities associated with each element are often termed elemental energies. It's important not to confuse these with the actual elementals, the elemental beings themselves. The following table may aid your understanding.

Element	Direction	Elementals	Elemental Energies (Qualities)
Air	East	Fairies, sylphs	Ideas, inspiration, imagination, creativity, to know
Fire	South	Salamanders, dragons	Passion, drive, ambition, motivation, to will
Water	West	Naiads, undines	Emotion, intuition, feeling, courage, to dare
Earth	North	Gnomes, elves	Steadfastness, dependability, commitment, self-control, to keep silent

All of these elemental energies work together and need each other to exist. Earth would be barren without light or water; fire could not burn without air. All are inextricably linked, and so it is in magick and circle casting. To ignore, or not call all four to create a balanced energy in your circle could result in creating the opposite magickal intent you were working for.

We see this very thing when the elemental energies are out of balance in someone's personality. Too much fire and they are angry and destructive. Too much air and they can't think clearly. Too much water and they are overly sensitive or adrift in a sea of emotions. Too much earth and they are unmotivated and can't seem to accomplish much.

The balance of the elements is very important to set your sacred space, so please do be mindful to invite them each individually, one at a time. Calling to them all simultaneously, without giving the proper attention, could very well make things interesting for you to say the least. The same goes for releasing; be mindful to address each energy specifically and escort them out.

Dismissing the elements and any invited elemental beings is not optional. Trust us, you don't want an unsupervised fire elemental running amok in your house!

Interesting note: You have elemental fingers. In the art of palmistry each finger represents, and transmits, a different elemental energy. Pinkie is air, ring is fire, middle is earth, and pointer is water. Your thumb is spirit. You may wish to point the corresponding finger to the direction you are welcoming, especially if you have not yet acquired and consecrated your athame (ritual blade).

The Quarters, or the Four Directions

In some groups or traditions, these are sometimes referred to as the corners. That said, the term "arc" might be a better description, as each joins seamlessly with the next to form a continuous circle.

Like the four seasons, the four elements, and the four energies, each space governs or houses everything associated with it. In fact, envisioning each direction as its own kingdom or home might make it easier to understand.

Again, the directions are: east—air; south—fire; west—water; north—earth.

In the kingdom of air, we should imagine springtime, early morning dew, pastel flowers, budding trees, the melting away of the winter, and the sun's light strengthening. It is a place of transformation and lightheartedness, a place where all kinds of things uplift and inspire us. We are enchanted by the laughter of playful fairies as the wind catches the sails of our imagination. However, we must be mindful to stay the course and not to be swept away to the place of fairy for fear that we might not return.

For the kingdom of fire, we should imagine summer in full tilt. The heat of the noonday sun beats down, warming our bones. Plants are filled with energy and fruits are ready for early harvesting. The animals born in the spring are now young adults full of vitality and looking for their own mates. This is a place filled with desire and strength, a place that houses dragons and salamanders, which positively crackles with excitement. Yet we must be careful to not be seduced by the power it holds.

The kingdom of water allows us to experience twilight, the liminal time between day and night. The sun's light has almost completely left the sky and we can sense the moonlight and all its mystery. This is the kingdom of the hidden and the occult, where we must trust our intuition and get in touch with our deepest feelings. Here the light is diminishing. Our thoughts turn inward; we see harvesting, preparation, and readying to go within for the coming dark of winter. This is the place of the mystical creatures of water and the undines. The call of the mystic is strong, but so is the siren's song. We must be wary not to be dashed upon the rocks by the swirling seas of our emotions.

In the kingdom of earth, we are grounded. This is the place of reality. The glass is neither half full nor half empty; it is simply half a glass. The seeds that are stored here remember exactly how to grow and what to be—they need no instruction. In this place it is midnight, the magickal time. Things may appear to be still and sleeping, but they are very much alive, awake and ready for all that is about to happen. Much hard work has been done in preparation and foundations have been laid, for all who dwell here—the gnomes, elves and wee folk—are great collectors and organizers. But even within this practical place, we must be mindful of the need for balance—to save for a rainy day is a good thing … to hoard, not so much.

The Watchtowers

The analogy we gave for envisioning each of the four directions as its own kingdom is not an accidental one, for, in common with many other groups (but by no means all) in our tradition, we do actually see each quarter as a kingdom, populated by elemental beings that are ruled over by an elemental king.

The entrance to each elemental kingdom is a portal or gateway between the physical and magickal worlds. And in our tradition, each gateway is guarded by a gatehouse known as a Watchtower.

We see the Watchtowers as large, fortified gatehouses, such as what you would find at the entrance to a castle.

The Watchtower's gates are made of huge, arched, oaken doors above which sits the symbol of that element. This is the doorway to that kingdom, the portal between the mundane and the magickal. Here, you may call forth energy from or set out on a quest to get to know their beings, energies, and everything they have to offer for your magickal work.

On top of each Watchtower sits a large brazier that is big enough to hold a large signal fire visible from a great distance. This is the fire that will be lit when you ask for the energy of that direction to find its way to your circle. Not only does the brazier light the way for the elementals—it also serves to honor the elemental king and the guardian of the Watchtower itself.

The Elemental Kings

While there is a general consensus on the names of the four kings, there is much disagreement on their spelling. What's more, no one seems to know for sure where they actually came from. There has been much speculation in High Magick that the names were derived from either Hebrew or Sanskrit. Some credit has been given to Éliphas Lévi, the Rosicrucians, or perhaps even the Hermetic Order of the Golden Dawn, but this is a story best left for another day.

The kingdom of air is the realm of the sylphs and/or fairies and their ruling king is named Paralda, which has been translated to mean "to bear," "to birth," or "to increase." In Hebrew, the word *peri* means "reward." He is known for his energies of both fertility and rebirth; remember springtime and the land coming back to life after the dead of winter.

In our tradition, he appears to us as a younger male, wearing the pastel colors of spring, and, many times, bright yellow shoes. He is clean-shaven, physically fit, and full of the joys of spring (pun intended).

That said, we would strongly recommend journeying through the Watchtower of the East and meeting him for yourself, especially if you are seeking inspiration and positive thoughts.

The kingdom of fire is commanded by Djin (also spelled Djiin, Djinn, and Djin'n). It is interesting to note that his name is similar to the Arabic word, *jinni*, which has been morphed into the "genie" of the English language.

While it's possible to get lost for hours thinking about the origins and meanings of esoteric words, it's best to be mindful to avoid the rabbit holes. Looking to Hebrew or Chaldean, we find the translation of the word *djin* to be more akin to law, judge, or justice. We consider Djin a more formal figure, much like that of the Emperor or the Justice trumps in the tarot. He is the epitome of authority, stern and unwavering—after all, he is the ruler of dragons, salamanders, and the unforgiving passion of fire.

The mysterious kingdom of water is ruled over by Nixsa (also spelled Nixa or Necksa). There are arguments for each spelling as well as whether this king is actually a queen, as the element of water is passive feminine. Most traditional groups tend to follow Lévi's writing and keep with the assignment of king.

Numerous suggestions have been made as to the meaning of this name, but for the sake of expediency, we have settled on "to weed" (as the element of water corresponds to the west, the time of harvest, and gateway to the ancestors), "to be concealed" (according to Lévi's translation, which makes sense as water hides what lies beneath), or "serpent," an ancient symbol for Scorpio, the fixed sign of water.

When we journey to meet him, Nixsa usually appears to us as fluid, undulating and amorphous—almost anything but a solid form.

He is the ruler of the undines, more mature and compassionate than the first two kings, yet ever so serious in his demeanor, for the nature of his job is to govern emotions, feelings, and the things that provoke them—not exactly an easy task.

The kingdom of earth is overseen by Ghob (also spelled Ghobe, or Gob). Please note this is pronounced *gobe*, as in "robe," and not *gahb*, with a short "o" sound. Be mindful that we are dealing with the energies of fixed earth, inflexible and unwavering—you really don't want to offend him.

The Hebrew translation used by the Hermetic Order of the Golden Dawn seems to point to "collector of money, curator, or keeper of fine things." This association makes sense, as Ghob is the ruler of the gnomes, mystical creatures renowned for their love of gold, crystals, and other earthly treasures. We see him as a wise and learned elder, a distinguished figure with a long white beard, clearly in possession of great knowledge and a firm grasp on reality.

It is very important to build a strong relationship with the energies and characters of each direction. To that end, we need to get you started on building an essential skill for the practicing Witch.

Elemental Meditation Exercises

Over the many years we have been raising Witches in our tradition, we have learned that some of the most valuable tools for deepening understanding are guided meditations that lead you on experiential astral journeys.

We strongly recommend keeping a magickal diary, something we refer to as a weirdness journal, to keep track of your explorations, findings, and general weirdness that takes place on your travels through the astral realms.

Find yourself a nice, quiet place where you won't be disturbed for a while—indoors or out, it matters not. Turn off or unplug your phone—the world won't end if you don't answer that call or respond to that text message immediately. You might even want to light some of your favorite incense to help set the mood.

If you have someone you can work with, you might find it useful to take turns reading the guided meditations to each other. If you don't have this luxury, you can always record yourself reading the meditation. Play it back and journey along.

Once you're sitting comfortably, we'll begin.

Close your eyes and relax … Become aware of your heartbeat and, as you relax even more, let your pulse slow and your psychic vision clear.

Take another deep breath and be present. Let all outside energy just fade away.

Take another deep breath and exhale slowly. A white mist fills the room; you feel it on your skin and in your hair. You begin to feel like you're floating.

You land on the edge of a beautiful dense forest. It's daybreak, and the sun is just rising, so you walk in that direction.

You come to what looks like a tower that is part of a lavish castle. It is round and has a large oak door. Over the door is the upward lined triangle, the symbol of air.

The door opens and the gatekeeper is King Paralda himself. Take a moment to look upon him and make mental note of how he has appeared to you.

He invites you in.

The place is alive with the energy of spring.

Think about what spring means for you: cool light, refreshing breezes, gentle showers, pastel flowers, budding trees, and bushes.

You can see what look like butterflies of all colors flitting around in the trees. They may look like butterflies, but you know they are fairies and sylphs.

Paralda invites you to take a seat on a small wooden bench beneath a large alder tree. You sit down and continue your survey of this magickal landscape. You take in the incredible sounds, sights, and smells that delight your senses.

As you look around, one of the beautiful winged creatures breaks away from the others and flies toward you. One of the fairies comes down to visit you.

Allow yourself to look closely upon it and commit their gender and color to memory.

Spend a little time in their company.

Before they turn to leave and rejoin the others, let your fairy know that you will return to this place and work magick with them.

Paralda takes your hand and gently leads you back to the gate.

Thank him for letting you visit and step out into the forest.

You notice now that it is reaching the peak of day and the sun has risen much higher in the sky, so you turn to follow it to the Watchtower of the South.

You come to what looks like a tower from a lavish castle. It is round and has a large oak door. Over the door is the upward triangle, the symbol of fire.

The door opens and the gatekeeper is King Djin himself. Take a moment to look upon him and make mental note of how he appears to you.

He invites you in. This place is very warm and filled with the smell of summer fruits and blossoms.

Think about what summer means for you—long days, green grass, social gatherings.

Djin invites you to take a seat on a small tree stump near a beautiful bonfire. You sit down and continue your survey of this magickal landscape. You take in the incredible sounds, sights, and smells that delight your senses.

As you look into the flames, you sense that the fire is somehow alive. Looking closer, you see movement in the living flames dancing around the burning coals.

Suddenly there is a sharp crack, and a glowing ember shoots up and out of the fire to land at your feet.

As the ember cools, it transforms into a beautiful salamander before your very eyes—the elemental being of fire.

Allow yourself to look closely upon it and commit their gender and color to memory. Spend a little time in their company.

Before they scurry away and rejoin the others playing in the flames, let your salamander know that you will return to this place and work magick with them.

When you are done, Djin takes your hand and leads you back to the gate. Thank him for letting you visit, and step into the forest once again.

It is evening, and the sun is now setting. You turn and follow it to the west.

You come to what looks like a tower from a lavish castle. It is round and has a large oak door. Over the door is the downward triangle, the symbol of water.

The door opens and the gatekeeper is King Nixsa himself. Take a moment to look upon him and make mental note of how he has appeared to you.

He invites you in. This place is filled with the smell of fall leaves and crisp air.

Think about what the fall means for you: harvest time, plentiful food, the time of the ancestors and magick.

Nixsa invites you to have a seat on a metal bench near a crystal clear and calm lake. You sit down and continue your survey of this magickal landscape. You take in the incredible sounds, sights, and smells that delight your senses.

As you gaze into the lake, you see movement in the water. Colored lights dart this way and that as they swim at different speeds.

Suddenly, one of the lights breaks the surface of the water and continues in a graceful arc to land at your feet.

Before your very eyes, it transforms into an undine—the elemental being of water. Allow yourself to look at it closely and commit their gender and color to memory.

Spend a little time in their company. Before they turn and gracefully dive back into the water, let your undine know that you will return to this place and work magick with them.

Nixsa takes your hand and leads you back to the gate. Thank him for letting you visit. Once again, step out into the forest.

Darkness has now fallen; the night sky is peppered with stars. Instinctively, you find the Big Dipper and trace a line between the two outer stars that points to the North Star, Polaris. You walk toward it, in the direction of the Watchtower of the North.

You come to what looks like a tower from a lavish castle. It is round and has a large oak door. Over the door is the downward lined triangle, the symbol of earth.

The door opens and the gatekeeper this time is King Ghob. Take a moment to look upon him and make mental note of how he has appeared to you.

He invites you in. The place is cold, dark, and very still. Ghob offers you a jacket to keep warm. You walk with him across freshly fallen snow to a small cave. You can hear all kinds of voices and noises coming from within.

Ghob invites you to have a seat on a small stone bench near the entrance of the cave. You sit down and continue your survey of this magickal landscape as your eyes adjust to the darkness. You take in the incredible sounds, sights, and smells that delight your senses.

As you look upon the cave, a gnome appears at the entrance, lantern in hand. You see this gnome stride purposefully out to meet you. Allow yourself to look closely upon it and commit their gender and color to memory.

Spend a little time in their company.

Before they turn and march back into the cave, let your gnome know that you will return to this place and work magick with them.

Ghob takes your hand and leads you back to the gate. Thank him for letting you visit. Step out into the forest once again.

It is still dark, but the sky is beginning to pale in anticipation of the coming dawn. The air is cold and crisp and your breath forms clouds of mist that hang in the air.

As you contemplate the swirling vapors, you realize that a fog has rolled in and is obscuring the landscape from view. It is cool and refreshing upon your skin.

You feel yourself gently lifted and transported back to the place you began your journey.

Take a deep, cleansing breath, and come back into your body. Tense and relax a few muscles and open your eyes when you are ready.

Congratulations and welcome back!

If you are new to astral journeywork, you may feel light-headed, dizzy, or even a tad nauseated. It may help to drink some water or hold a grounding crystal such as hematite. Certainly don't drive or operate heavy machinery until you're fully back in your body.

Be sure to write down your experiences in your weirdness journal, and feel free to visit again. In fact, we strongly recommend that you do so in order to become familiar with the energies to which you are calling and, ultimately, working your magick.

The Guardians of the Watchtowers

This chapter would not be complete without mention of the Guardians; those who watch over the portals between the mundane and magickal worlds and whatever resides or operates within the magickal realms—including those mortals who would dare enter.

Within the circles of High Magick, it is common knowledge, albeit largely unspoken, that the guardians are actually archangels, namely Uriel, Gabriel, Raphael, and Michael.

Yes, we did say "archangels," but hold on a second. Before you cast this book aside in a fit of pique brought about by a deep-seated aversion to all things Christian, please understand that High Magick has its roots in Judaic mysticism, which predates Christianity by at least two thousand years. We would also ask you to consider the fact that we humans have a sorely limited perception of reality, and as such, are consumed by an innate need to personify almost everything in order to make it fit the constructs of our understanding.

Perhaps if you consider an angel to be a manifestation of sentient energy within the apparent world, rather than an eight-foot-tall winged being able to float through walls, it may sit easier with you. Whichever way you choose to see it, you must agree that to encounter an archangel in person is likely to be an awe-inspiring experience that may necessitate a change of underwear.

Setting controversy aside for a moment, focusing purely on the established teachings doesn't really help too much either. Sadly, the whole subject is as clear as mud, to borrow a phrase. It is certainly possible to hold a lengthy debate as to which archangel belongs with which direction; in fact, if we look at the revealed religions, we can see this issue has ruffled feathers for a very long time. The Kabalistic teachings see Uriel as Sandalphon and/or Metatron, but their elemental assignments are not really clear as they are often depicted as working together in a specific sphere or sharing an elemental energy—something that's not exactly helpful for Wiccan ritual workings.

If we look toward the writings of the Hermetic Order of the Golden Dawn, we can see that as studious high magicians, they have applied some very serious thought to the matter. Although the original

Hermetic Order of the Golden Dawn (founded by Freemasons William Robert Woodman, William Wynn Westcott, and Samuel Liddell MacGregor Mathers) ceased to exist in 1908, it was reestablished in 1977 under the mentorship of Israel Regardie, who claimed initiatory lineage to the original order.

Even though the Hermetic Order of the Golden Dawn has established temples in many countries around the world, they remain a very private organization with membership by invitation only. Nonetheless, Chic Cicero and Sandra Tabatha Cicero, prolific authors and adepts of the Order, have created a valuable online resource that provides an excellent insight into the order's teachings.[4] The website also contains the original artwork of Sandra Tabatha Cicero, which you may find helpful in visualizing the Archangels in the manner the Order describes.

They consider Raphael to be the great archangel of the element of air, whose name means "Healer of God." For them, Raphael is seated in the east, and visualized as a tall, fair figure standing upon the clouds in robes of yellow and violet. He is holding the Caduceus of Hermes as a symbol of his intellectual, healing powers.

Next is Michael, seated in the south, considered the great archangel of the element of fire, whose name means "Perfect One of God." Michael is visualized as a manly figure, dressed in armor or robes of red and green. Vanquisher of evil and protector of humanity, he stands in the pose of a warrior surrounded by flames, and pictured holding either a sword or a spear—as both are forged in fire and strongly connected to its energies.

Next is Gabriel, the great archangel of the element of water, whose name means "Strong One of God." Holding a chalice of water

---

4. Official website of the Hermetic Order of the Golden Dawn, https://www .hermeticgoldendawn.org.

as a symbol of the creative, fertile powers of consciousness in all its forms, Gabriel is placed in the west, and visualized standing upon the waters of the sea, dressed in robes of blue and orange.

Finally, Uriel (sometimes called Auriel) is considered to be the great archangel of the element of earth, whose name means "the Light of God."

Planted firmly in the north, Uriel is pictured as rising up from the foliage which grows from the earth. He holds stems of ripened wheat and wears clothes of gold, bronze, green, and black.

While these assignments are perfectly plausible and have been in the public domain for some appreciable time, we do strongly recommend that you visit each archangel for yourself and ask them where they are to be seated in your circle. But how does one visit an archangel?

Well, the good news is there is an easily accessible and powerful visual tool that will help you. Cast your mind back to 1909 or thereabouts, when a certain Arthur Edward Waite was working to publish his new tarot deck with illustrations by Pamela Colman-Smith.

The pair had met each other through their membership of the Hermetic Order of the Golden Dawn, and it is perhaps unsurprising that the tarot deck on which they collaborated reveals a great many of the secret teachings within the order, albeit hidden within plain sight.

It is interesting to note that the four archangels are depicted within the major arcana of the Rider-Waite-Smith tarot:

Michael is Temperance (XIV), assigned as Sagittarius (fire), or to some readers, Cancer (water).

Raphael appears on the Lovers (VI). This trump is Gemini (air) and depicted presiding over the Garden of Eden and Mount Zion.

Gabriel is seen on the Judgement card (XX) and represents the sign of Scorpio (water).

TEMPERANCE.

THE LOVERS.

JUDGEMENT.

THE DEVIL.

And last, but certainly not least, Uriel is hidden, again in plain sight. He is the Light or "Lux," the fallen angel, and appears on the Devil card (XV) as temptation or Capricorn (earth).

You may notice that even here, there is no definitive elemental assignment. Nonetheless, you could do far worse than use these tarot cards as visual cues for your astral journeywork.

Exercise: Tarot Meditation

As before, go to your comfortable place where you won't be disturbed for a while and simply gaze at your chosen tarot card until your vision blurs a little. Allow yourself to become lost within the card; allow the subliminal imagery within the illustration to speak directly to your subconscious mind.

Be sure to note your findings in your weirdness journal. And don't be surprised if your experiences differ widely from the established teachings.

We would also say that with their vast knowledge and love for all, archangels could not be restricted to just one element or gender—they are not human; they are pure, incomprehensible energy and only take on a humanlike form within the tiny space of our minds, just like everything else we humans need to personify in order to comprehend. Perhaps that is why the Kabbalists choose to blend them, but we don't know for sure. What we do know for sure is that, for your magick and practice to work, their directional assignments have to make sense to *you*.

The following exercise may help make your decision as to which guardian belongs with which direction.

Sit in a quiet place where you will not be interrupted. Have your weirdness journal and a pen handy, or at the very least, a piece of scrap paper to mark down your findings.

When doing this meditation, bear in mind that not everyone is visual, but most everyone can feel.

Close your eyes and first allow yourself to be immersed in the color yellow. Let it fill the entire eastern corner of the room.

If you can see it or imagine the color yellow on the backs of your eyelids, all the better; if not, that's okay too … just allow yourself to feel the color. Think of all the things associated with yellow: spring, fertility, dawn, fairies, King Paralda, and so on. Picture them and really focus on how spring makes you feel. Imagine the dawn and the sunrise, feel the anticipation and inspiration, know all that is east … the energy of air.

Now move to the south and fill that space with red. Again, you may not be able to actually see the color but we know how red feels— warm, passionate, and driven. Think of the noonday sun warming you, your desires and passions. Think of the king of the dragons and salamanders, Djin. Feel the color red all around you—how does it make you feel? Will yourself to be filled with the strength of the sun.

Now gently allow your awareness to move to the west and fill that space with beautiful blue light … the most beautiful blue light you have ever seen. Let yourself feel this light and flow in its energy. Dare to immerse yourself in the healing water, think of the fall, the harvest, your ancestors, and the Mysteries. Think of the king of the undines, Nixsa.

Slowly turn your attention to the north, the stable grounding element of earth. Fill that space with the color green. Think about this space, mountains, caves, open space, huge fields of tilled earth. Listen to its silence. Let yourself be quiet and safe. Think of the king of the gnomes, Ghob.

Now call upon one archangel at a time and let yourself feel where they belong within your circle, where they are most comfortable.

Michael—God's protector; Gabriel—God's strength; Raphael—God's healer; and Uriel—God's light. What feels right to you?

Maybe you notice the direction they seem to come from or a color they are covered in. It's possible that you might also notice sounds or scents that serve to reinforce the sense of direction to which they belong. Make note of this very personal discovery and use these directions as your assigned directions for the guardians within your sacred space.

The Lights of the Watchtowers

If you cast your mind back to the beginning of this chapter, we made mention of the braziers sitting on top of the turrets of the Watchtowers. You will recall that these hold signal fires that are lit when you call upon the energies of that direction, to light the way for the elemental beings and to honor the elemental king and the Guardian of the Watchtower itself.

So how exactly does one go about lighting these? Like many things in the arts magickal, we use a physical object in the mundane world to represent its counterpart in the magickal world. This is known as sympathetic magick. In our tradition, we use candles to represent the lights of the Watchtowers. As we call to each direction and light the candle, we visualize lighting the signal fire within the brazier.

While you could certainly use a regular white candle for each of the directions, it might be a better idea to select a candle that is an appropriate color for each quarter.

| East (air)—Yellow | South (fire)—Red |
| North (earth)—Green | West (water)—Blue |

Although we will cover this in much greater detail in the chapter on magickal tools, you should be aware that these candles represent the lights of the Watchtowers and *not* the element itself. It would be both highly impractical and hugely insulting to expect that a water elemental would be comfortable residing within a burning candle.

Summary

In this chapter, we have introduced you to the elements, the very foundation of both the magickal world and your training in the arts magickal.

You have journeyed to the Watchtowers, met the elemental kings, and interacted with the elemental beings who reside within these magickal realms. Now imagine these four kingdoms: air's territory bordering the lands of earth and fire, and water's realm bordering those of fire and earth. Together, they are the four directions, the four seasons that form the Wheel of the Year, and four wedges of the same circle—a circle you can create anywhere by simply inviting in their energies.

Now that you have a working relationship and a good understanding of the elements and all they have to offer, you are ready to continue your journey onward.

four

The Sabbats

In this chapter, we go over the sabbats: eight spokes of the constantly turning Wheel of the Year and the principal holy days celebrated by Witches the world over. Not only do we discuss the origins and significance of each sabbat; we also provide practical examples you can use in ritual to honor the Wheel's turning.

In the Craft, we observe eight special days or times that bring change to nature. These days are seen as markers for their seasons. There are four solar sabbats, belonging to the God, that mark the changes in the sun's light, and four terrestrial sabbats that belong to the Goddess or Earth Mother. In the next chapter, we talk about how the Goddess connects to the moon and its eight phases, but for now, let's explore the sun's journey through the eight sabbats and how this passage affects our living world.

The solar sabbats are actually termed the lesser sabbats, which may seem a little odd when these are still recognized in the common calendar as the beginning of the seasons. As Witches, however, we tend to acknowledge a greater connection to the earth than the sun, for we are born of the earth and will return to her at the end of our days. As is said in the Charge of the Goddess: "From me, all things proceed, and to me, they must return."[5]

Within the Craft, these sabbats are most commonly known as Yule, Ostara, Litha, and Mabon, although in our tradition we refer to them by their Welsh names: Alban Arthan, Alban Eilir, Alban Hefin, and Alban Elfed.

Looking to their dates, Yule is the winter solstice, Ostara the spring or vernal equinox, Litha the summer solstice, and Mabon the autumnal equinox. In the common calendar, these dates fall on the first day of the season and are most often celebrated on or near the twenty-first day of the month in which they occur: Spring—March 21; Summer—June 21; Autumn—September 21; and Winter—December 21.

For the most part these solar (or lesser) sabbats are associated with the God, although Ostara is actually a sun goddess. Therefore, it's not surprising that the other four terrestrial sabbats are called greater sabbats and are generally associated with the Goddess.

Oddly enough, we actually use the sun's position to mark the greater sabbats as well. Because they are so strongly connected to the earth, they're often viewed as agricultural sabbats. Within Wiccan circles, they are most commonly known as Imbolc, Beltane, Lughnasadh, and Samhain, although in our tradition we refer to them by their Welsh names: Gwyl Ffraid, Calan Haf (or Calan Mai), Gwyl Awst, and Calan Gaeaf.

In our tradition, we celebrate these on the cross-quarters, the point where the sun is exactly midway between the solar sabbats. This is also where the sun reaches the middle of the four fixed signs of the Zodiac: Gwyl Ffraid (Imbolc) occurs when the sun is in Aquarius, Calan Haf (Beltane) in Taurus, Gwyl Awst (Lughnasadh) in Leo, and Calan Gaeaf (Samhain) in Scorpio.

---

5. Valiente, *Charge of the Goddess.*

The sun travels through all twelve signs of the zodiac in a year, moving at a rate of one degree per day, thereby taking thirty days to transit the thirty degrees of each sign. Given that each astrological sign most commonly begins around the twenty-first day of the month, the midway point (fifteen degrees) typically occurs around the seventh day of the following month. While this is the case for our tradition, it should be noted that for many other groups, the sabbats are commonly observed near the first day of the month in which they occur.

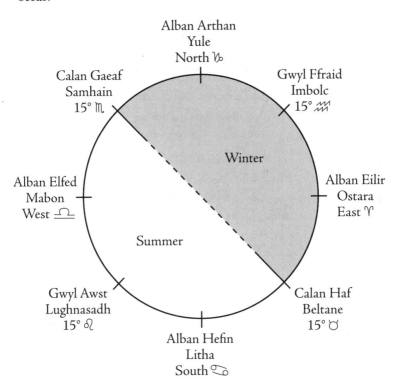

Within the Craft, the greater sabbats mark the true start of the seasons, while the solar sabbats mark the common or cowan seasons.

Consider the date of June 21 (or thereabouts), where the sun is directly over the Tropic of Cancer. In the northern hemisphere, this is the summer solstice, the point where astronomical summer is "maxed out." Here, the sun is at the peak of his power; he has climbed to his zenith in the sky and the days are at their longest—tomorrow he will resume his inevitable journey along the ecliptic, back toward the equator, and the days will shorten.

In the Craft, we celebrate Alban Hefin (Litha), or Midsummer's Day, while in the secular world, this is only considered the beginning of summer. Yet, many Wiccans have already celebrated the beginning of summer around May Eve with the fires of Beltane (Calan Haf).

You may have noticed that the Welsh name of each solar sabbats begins with *alban*, which roughly translates to "height," "light," "brilliance," or "peak"; hence "Alban" indicates the midpoint or height of the season, whereas the terrestrial sabbats begin with *calan* or *gwyl*, "first" or "feast," marking the beginning of the season.

The four solar or lesser sabbats mark the peak of each season, and the four terrestrial or greater sabbats are held on the cross-quarters between them to mark the end of one season and the beginning of the next. Together, they form the eight spokes of the Wheel of the Year.

But where or when does the Wheel begin? The start of the year has been a subject of much conjecture ever since we as humans began to measure time. In pure astrological terms, the year begins as the sun enters Aries, an event that coincides with the spring equinox. Many early calendars were also tied to the cycles of the moon as, like the length of the day, the changing phases of the moon were easy to observe. Even to this day, the date of Easter is calculated as the first

Yule
Midwinter's Night
Winter Solstice
longest night
Alban Arthan

Samhain
Halloween
Celtic New Year
Calan Gaeaf

December 21*
Sun enters Capricorn

October 31**
Begin Celtic Winter

February 2**
Begin Celtic Spring

Imbolc
Candle Mas
Gwyl Ffraid

Mabon
Autumnal Equinox
equal day/night
Alban Elfed

September 21*
Sun enters Libra

March 21*
Sun enters Aries

Eostar
Spring Equinox
equal day/night
Alban Eilir

August 1**
Begin Celtic Autumn

Sun enters Cancer
June 21*

May 1**
Begin Celtic Summer

Lammas
Lughnasadh
Gwyl Awst

Beltane
Mayday
Calan Haf

Litha
Midsummer's Night
Summer Solstice
longest day
Alban Hefin

Sunday following the first full moon after the spring equinox. Although this date moves from year to year, it averages to around April 1. Various popes and emperors have tweaked the calendar somewhat since, but this time was widely considered the start of the agricultural year, as the danger of frost had passed and planting could begin in earnest. When the official start of the year was moved to January 1, many folks living in rural areas continued to follow the agricultural year for some appreciable time, presumably because word of the change had not yet reached them—hence the term "April Fool."

For many Wiccan groups, however, the Wheel begins at Beltane (May Eve), the beginning of summer (Calan Haf). In our tradition, in common with many others who follow a Celtic path, our new year begins at Calan Gaeaf (Samhain), or summer's end.

The early Celts divided the year into light (summer) and dark (winter) halves. In the same way that the day began at sunset, the year began at the end of summer at sunset on Calan Gaeaf (Samhain).

Although we cover each sabbat in greater detail later in this chapter, you may find the following table helpful in becoming familiar with the dates for each sabbat.

Sabbat	Approx. Date	Position on Wheel of the Year
Samhain (Calan Gaeaf)	October 31	Beginning of winter, Celtic New Year
Yule (Alban Arthan)	December 21	Winter solstice, Midwinter's Night (longest night)
Imbolc (Gwyl Ffraid)	February 1	Beginning of spring, Feast of Brid (Ffraid)
Ostara (Alban Eilir)	March 21	Spring equinox, Mid-spring
Beltane (Calan Haf)	May 1	Beginning of summer, May Eve
Litha (Alban Hefin)	June 21	Summer solstice, Midsummer's Day (Longest Day)
Lughnasadh (Gwyl Awst)	August 1	Beginning of autumn, feast of Lugh (August), grain harvest
Mabon (Alban Elfed)	September 21	Autumnal equinox, Mid-autumn

Cast your mind back to the last chapter for a moment and consider the four elemental kingdoms as the four seasons which make up the Wheel of the Year. The boundaries between the kingdoms are not hard, fixed lines. Rather, there is a blurring between them as the north gradually yields to the east and relinquishes its grip on winter to give way to the coming spring.

In exactly the same way, the Wheel of the Year should be seen as a whole and not just eight, unrelated days. It is a woven, living, breathing, ever-changing energy. As it turns, it tells us the story of dark and light, our own lives, and the journey of the God and Goddess.

When we first set out on this path, it can be somewhat unclear and more than a little confusing as to how their story actually works.

We are asked to see the God as the Son, the Hunter, and the Sage, and the Goddess as the Maiden, the Mother, and the Crone.

We are supposed to see their relationship ebb and flow, change and grow, but it can be a daunting and rather confusing task: How can he be her son, her lover, and her god? How can she be his mother, his consort, and his goddess? It certainly doesn't help matters that in our self-serving, artificially lit, climate-controlled culture, we seem to be programmed all backward. The ancient Celts would slow down and begin a time of retreat for the winter due to the lack of light, the intense cold, and meager food rations. They most certainly would not be caught up in the "holiday hype" and months of indulging. Instead we believe that the dark time provided the ideal opportunity to learn from past mistakes while eagerly preparing for the return of the sun. By contrast, in the peak of the summer sun, ancient Celts would have been working hard to make best possible use of all the bountiful gifts the earth had bestowed on them … *not* frittering away the precious hours of daylight on vacation, sipping margaritas on the beach.

We could learn a lot if we paid more attention to the natural rhythms of the Wheel. As we progress on this path, hopefully we will begin to recognize the grand dance that takes place: the Earth's cycles, the ebb and flow of the universe, and how all this affects us.

There's a chant used in almost all our rituals, adapted from the wisdom inscribed upon the Emerald Tablet by Hermes Trismegistus: "As above, so below; as within, so without; as the Universe, so the soul." It eloquently conveys the concept of how the macrocosm and microcosm are inextricably linked, and that we are all part of the universe, singing in praise of itself.

Although you may be somewhat familiar with the sabbats, we do ask that you try to see these eight festivals in new and different ways as you read. You could consider them as four sabbats and their reflections across the Wheel, or perhaps examine them as just the light and dark halves of the year.

Look deeper and you will truly know this wonderful, natural way of life. Look again until you feel it click within you, and then know that every time you reach the same sabbat on the next turn of the Wheel, you will see even more.

For us, even after some twenty-five years of leading sabbat rites, we most always see something that gives us a new perspective and an even deeper connection to the nature of nature itself.

Remember, above all, that to understand the Mysteries, you must experience them. We invite you to lock arms and join the intricate and beautiful dance with ourselves, the Lord and Lady, and the sun, moon, and stars.

The Sabbat Rites

In our tradition, we follow a Welsh-Celtic pantheon and refer to our sabbats by their Welsh names. It is interesting to note that Welsh is a far more descriptive language than English; the very words serve to illustrate concepts and features.

Although Welsh is not our native language, we will endeavor to explain the meanings of the Welsh names that may help you to understand the true nature of the sabbats.

You may also notice that some of the stories bear more than a passing resemblance to more modern, revealed religions, such as Christianity. Understand that the sabbats are the story of the Earth, the sun, and of life itself. They are as old as time—in fact, they *are* time, for it is the movement of the Earth around the sun, and the moon around the Earth, that defines our days, weeks, months, and years.

Not surprising, then, that these understandings have been adopted and adapted by other beliefs to fit the constructs of their dogma.

A Note about the Rituals

Within this chapter, we have included practical examples you could use as part of your ritual to honor or celebrate a particular sabbat. These are not complete rituals themselves but are designed to be inserted into your circle format at the appropriate place. If you stick with it, you should be able to comfortably create and perform rituals for almost any occasion by the time you get to the end of this book.

Yule or the Winter Solstice

Welsh Name: Alban Arthan—White, Light, or Height of the Bear

Time Marked: Midwinter's night—the longest night

Short Meaning: The sun's return

The Lore

This sabbat marks the birth of the sun god (as opposed to the son of God). Note that the newborn sun is called the Child of Promise at this time of year.

Calan Gaeaf (Samhain) ushered in the dark time of winter; all was still, withdrawn, and quiet. But now there is a divine spark, a light, a new hope, and the promise of lengthening days and warmer weather.

The Holly King, who took over the dark half of the solar year at Alban Hefin (Litha), now must fight a losing battle and surrender his reign of darkness. He must return the crown to his brother, the Oak King, the ruler and caretaker of the light.

The Goddess, who had shown us death in life at the summer solstice, now awakens us to life in death as she gives birth to the spark of all life.

The invincible sun has conquered death and is now resurrected as the god of grain, bread, sustenance, and responsibility. He awakens to bring back the light, to rejuvenate us, help us plan for the coming year, and symbolizes the hopes of all that is to be.

The wheel turns; ebb becomes flow. We are now in our waxing phase, growing toward the promise of spring and Gwyl Ffraid (Imbolc).

Ritual

You may wish to add holly, mistletoe, ivy, pine boughs, or other traditional greenery to your altar for this ritual. You could make a bouquet or place them on the floor around the base of your altar to form a wreath (itself a symbol of the Wheel).

On this night, after the circle is cast, we darken the space completely for the lighting of the Yule log. The log should be oak or birch with places for eight candles to represent the sabbats, one black (Samhain), one white (Yule), three red for the solar sabbats (Ostara, Litha, Mabon) and three green for the terrestrial (Imbolc, Beltane, Lughnasadh).

Place the black candle, for Samhain, in the left of the middle two holes, and the white, for Yule, in the right. Then, in the holes to the left of the black candle (Samhain), place two red candles with a green in the middle, and in the holes to the right of the white candle (Yule), place two green with a red in the middle.

When complete, your Yule log should look like this:

Red	Green	Red	Black	White	Green	Red	Green
Litha	Lughnasadh	Mabon	Samhain	Yule	Imbolc	Ostara	Beltane

Symbolize the return of the sun by lighting the white candle first, and then moving to the right, light the green, red, and green candles. Next, move to the far left of the log and, again proceeding to the right, light the red, green, and red candles. Do not light the black candle—it is left dark so as not to disturb the ancestors.

You could also bring out the clear quartz you empowered at Alban Hefin (Litha) to capture the sun's light at its peak, and sing "return, return" just before the lighting of the Yule log.

While it might be confusing to refer to events that occur at a point on the Wheel we haven't actually come to yet, we have to jump on somewhere! After all, continually turning without beginning or end is what a wheel does.

In our tradition, we perform a mythic play that portrays the battle between the Holly King and Oak King; it represents the light's return and its symbolic victory over the reign of darkness.

Helpful Tips

You can burn the candles of your Yule log each day until they are gone to welcome the growing light.

You may also want to leave your crystals out of their pouch on your altar, to honor the Sun God and his reign during the light time of the year, before charging them up again at Alban Hefin (Litha).

Imbolc or Candlemas

Welsh Name: Gwyl Ffraid—The Festival of Brid

Time Marked: First day of spring

Short Meaning: Wake up Mother Earth and spring cleaning

The Lore

This festival is most commonly held around February 2. In the Christian calendar, it is celebrated as Candlemas, the symbolic return of the light.

As Witches, we understand that Yule marks the shortest day, and that going forward until Litha, the sun and the God's power are growing. But, with the worst of the winter still ahead of us, it's hard to actually see it.

However, at Imbolc we can truly feel the light increasing. With each passing day, the sun is climbing a little higher in the sky and the shadows are definitely receding. It seems to be brighter, and the sun feels a bit warmer on our skin. We can sense the stirring, or quickening, of nature responding to this light.

Imbolc has been variously translated to mean "in the belly" or "in milk" as a reference to lambing time. In the days long before the advent of Christianity, this festival was celebrated with balefires in an act of sympathetic magick to help warm and wake the sleeping earth. Perhaps this tradition has carried over to modern times with the burning of Yule trees.

Although the sabbat is often celebrated with fire, we should be mindful that this is also the birth of spring. We have crossed the border and entered the Kingdom of Air. Also at this time of year, the sun is in the sign of Aquarius. Consider all the energies that are at play: new beginnings, ideas, thoughts, and inspiration. Now is a great time to be making plans and starting new projects.

In our tradition, this sabbat is called Gwyl Ffraid. As mentioned before, *gwyl* is Welsh for "festival" (or "feast day"), and *Ffraid* is how Brid (pronounced *breed*, also known as Brigit, or Brigid) is known in Wales.

Brid is the Celtic goddess of the hearth and home and is also the root of the word "bride." She embodies the qualities of healing, poetry and smithcraft, and is often portrayed in triple-goddess form of Maiden, Mother, and Crone, with her maiden aspect tending a forge.

She is a feminine bard, seer, and walker between the worlds, working to preserve the old ways and their stories.

As her totem animals are the cow and ewe, it is not hard to see how she is connected to this birthing time of year, for both cow and ewe would be in milk.

Although the sun/God truly challenges the darkness and cold of winter at this time, the moon/Goddess is also honored with this terrestrial sabbat; we celebrate her as the giver of life, light, and abundance. As the Wheel turns, the Crone of the long dark winter fades, and the Maiden of spring re-emerges.

Imbolc is also a time of spring cleaning and a cleansing fire is usually lit, not just to keep warm, but to clear away all the debris and detritus left over from the forced internment of the winter months.

Typically, you would burn your Yule tree or any leftover nubs of candles and used magickal items such as herbs, bits of cloth, or finished spell work.

Sweep, sweep, sweep away and renew your energies in the coming light. You could also use your broom to bless the ground and then jump as high as you can to encourage your crops to grow.

Ritual

We see Gwyl Ffraid (Imbolc) as the first day of spring and our goal is to help turn the Wheel toward warmer weather and fertility for the land.

As one might expect in a festival named for her, Ffraid (Brid) plays a large part in our ritual. Gwyl Ffraid (Imbolc) is the time for charging her bed and banishing winter. In an act of sympathetic magick, a phallic symbol is placed inside the bed to fertilize the land.

Create Ffraid's (Brid's) bed with some branches of fir on a silver plate or in a small flat basket.

Feel the energy you are calling flow through you and out into the bed, readying it for the fertilization.

Using your own wand or one fashioned from a short stick and a pine cone, visualize the fertile energies of the god welling up inside it.

Once you feel both the bed and the wand are ready, bring them together. Place the wand inside the bed and feel the fertile, creative forces unite, bringing forth hope and positive intention.

As you place the wand inside the bed, you may wish to speak these words:

> Thus we banish winter,
> thus we welcome spring.
> Say farewell to what is dead,

and greet each living thing.
Thus we banish winter,
thus we welcome spring.

Helpful Tips

In your sabbat working for Gwyl Ffraid (Imbolc), you may want to read aloud the Charge of the Goddess. We've included this in full in chapter 8. As you do so, prepare yourself to welcome the spring and Ffraid (Brid) herself for positive energy, growth, and prosperity in your life.

Now is a great time to make plans for projects you can start as the days get warmer, such as planting your herb garden.

Ostara or Eostre

Welsh Name: Alban Eilir—Light, or Height of Earth

Time Marked: Vernal equinox

Short Meaning: Fertility and balance

The Lore

This solar sabbat occurs around March 21, when the sun is directly overhead the equator. This is known as an equinox, a time where the hours of night and day are in balance. But remember, the Wheel is waxing, so think spring. Earth is at its most fertile and life is bursting forth ... flowers, eggs, and bunnies abound.

At this time, the sun rises directly in the east. It's therefore hardly a wonder that almost all the festivals celebrated by the various religions take their name from this direction ... Ostara (*Ost* is German for "east"), Eostre, Easter, and so on.

It's worth pointing out that although this is a solar (or lesser) sabbat and is most commonly associated with the sun/God, Ostara is actually a goddess. She is actually one of quite a few goddesses associated with the sun. Her name is cognate with Eostre; honored by the Germanic Anglo-Saxons of early medieval Britain who held feasts in her honor at this time of year, welcoming the growing light of spring.

In Old English, the fertility goddess's name became *Eastre*, from which we derive the names of the female reproductive hormone, estrogen, and the Christian festival Easter.

Easter is when Christians celebrate the resurrection of Christ, and as is common with many of their holy days, it too has Pagan origins. Even the date of its celebration is based on the first Sunday after the first full moon following the equinox.

With the passing of the equinox, the length of daylight now exceeds the length of night. The light of the God, his sun (son), has overthrown the powers of darkness and life begins anew. He is risen from the dead (of winter). That aside, have you ever wondered what Easter eggs and bunnies have to do with the resurrection of Christ? The equinox is a signal to all the creatures of Earth that the winter no longer poses a threat to their young and they begin to multiply; rabbits start to breed, and birds lay an abundance of eggs.

When our ancestors emerged from their dwellings, following the forced imprisonment of winter, food supplies were seriously low or had been completely exhausted, and they were hungry—very hungry. Fortunately, as the birds had started laying, eggs were plentiful, nutritious, and easy to obtain. So, our ancestors set out to search for them. It has been suggested that this is the true origin of the modern-day Easter egg hunt.

In the folklore associated with Eostre, we are told that Rabbit (sacred to the moon/Goddess and himself a symbol of fertility) wanted to please the goddess Eostre, so he found the best fertility symbol he could think of: an egg. He offered brightly colored ones as gifts to her.

Ritual

Ostara is when we honor the mother, celebrate spring, and empower thoughts and seeds for fertility as we dream of what will come.

Whatever seeds you may have saved from last year's harvest or purchased for this year's garden can now be blessed for fertility and good fortune.

Place the seeds packets in a basket for charging. Look at your collection and imagine each seed filled with potential and the energy of the guardians and devas of their plants. Point your athame or your pointer finger into the basket and say these words:

> May the powers of the ancient ones, source of all cre-
> ation, bless this time, this place, and all gathered here.
>
> May the powers of the Goddess, bright lady of the
> moon bless this time, this place, and all gathered here.
>
> And may the God, antlered hunter of the sun bless
> this time, this place, and all gathered here.
>
> May the powers of the guardian spirits, rulers of the
> elemental realms, bless this time, this place, and all gath-
> ered here.
>
> May the powers of the stars above and the Earth
> below, bless this time, this place, and all gathered here.
>
> So mote it be!

Helpful Tips

After this blessing of spring, plant some of your seeds in window boxes, propagators, or even a greenhouse if you are so lucky, and have little plants all ready for summer.

Beltane

Welsh Name: Calan Haf or Calan May—First day of May or summer

Time Marked: First day of summer

Short Meaning: The sacred marriage

The Lore

This sabbat is most commonly known as Beltane and is generally celebrated on or about May 1. Representative of the sacred marriage between the Lord of the Green Wood and the Queen of May, the sun god assumes his responsibilities for the land and fertility. Together, they bring forth new life at this time.

Beltane sits on the opposite side of the Wheel from Samhain— Calan Gaeaf (the first day of winter). It is a time of quickening, the first day of summer. Our thoughts turn outward as we look forward to the longer days and warm evenings summer promises.

Fire again plays a role, but as this is a terrestrial sabbat, we look to the land as well as the sky.

Our ancestors lit two fires in honor of the Great Ones and then jumped over or passed between them to ensure fertility throughout the land. Even cattle and livestock were led between the balefires to purify and bless the coming season's growth.

This sabbat also included the dance of the May Pole (an obvious phallic symbol). The pole represents the God and the ribbons and flowers represent the Goddess. As the ritual dance was performed, the ribbons were woven around the pole, symbolically reenacting their union.

At this time of great fertility, there was much merriment, carousing, and cavorting. The younger folks might also join with their prospective mate. But not until more than a year later would they wed, thus ensuring the partner they chose was indeed fertile.

In our tradition, we call this sabbat by its Welsh name, Calan Haf or Calan Mai. In the Celtic calendar, the day begins at sunset, hence many festivities start the evening before. In Wales, May Eve, or *Nos Galan Mai*, is still widely celebrated to this day. It is an *Ysbrydnos* (pronounced *Uh-sbrid-nos*) or "night of spirits," where the veil between this world and the world of fairy is at its thinnest, and mischief abounds.

Ritual

In our tradition, we tend to go all out for this sabbat. We gather the nine sacred woods: birch, oak, rowan, willow, hawthorn, hazel, apple, vine, fir, and elder, which we burn in two cauldrons (with the exception of elder, which should never be burnt).

Then we walk between the two fires to release old, unwanted energies and to bless and cleanse us as we move forward into summer.

We next do a broom-jumping rite—a mythic roleplay of the marriage of the God and Goddess—and we all dance the May Pole to honor their marriage and to ensure fertility for the coming year.

Since it would be difficult to have you dance the May Pole by yourself, you may wish to gather the sacred woods and burn them in two cauldrons, or other suitable containers.

Don't worry if you can't find the exact woods. Remember this is an act of sympathetic magick, so you can use any twigs you can find to represent the nine sacred woods.

Once your fires are going, you can walk between them with the intention of cleansing and blessing yourself and moving forward.

Because of your location, it may not be possible for you to collect the actual woods. However, you can always recite the chant and burn candles in the cauldrons to represent the balefires.

Again, the nine woods you need are birch, oak, rowan, willow, hawthorn, hazel, apple, vine, fir, and elder. Although you are collecting nine, you will only be burning eight—despite what the chant says:

> Nine woods in the Cauldron go, burn them fast and burn them slow.[6]

In fairness, it does go on to clarify:

> Birch in the fire goes to represent what the Lady knows.
> Oak in the forest towers with might, in the fire it brings the God's insight.
> Rowan is a tree of power causing life and magick to flower.
> Willows at the waterside stand ready to help us to the Summerland.
> Hawthorn is burned to purify and to draw faerie to your eye.

---

6. Herman Slater, ed. *Earth Religion* News—Vol. 1, 1974, *The Wiccan Rede*, (New York: E.R.N., 1974).

Hazel, the tree of wisdom and learning, adds its strength to the bright fire burning.

White are the flowers of apple tree that brings us fruits of fertility.

Grapes grow upon the vine, giving us both joy and wine.

Fir does mark the evergreen to represent immortality seen.

Elder is the Lady's tree—burn it not or cursed you'll be.

Helpful Tips

The elder tree has long been associated with the Goddess. In the spring, it bursts into life with bright green shoots and leaves along with an abundance of white flowers—the Goddess as Maiden. In late summer, it is laden with dark red berries—the Goddess as Mother. And in winter, nothing looks quite as old as its gnarled, twisted branches—the Goddess as Crone.

Moreover, the sap of the elder is red, so the tree appears to bleed when cut. Small wonder that elder was, and still is, so deeply revered.

Litha or the Summer Solstice

Welsh Name: Alban Hefin—Light, White, or Height of the Boar

Time Marked: Midsummer's Day

Short Meaning: Fruit harvest

The Lore

Midsummer is celebrated on or about June 21, as the sun is overhead the Tropic of Cancer, the most northerly point of the ecliptic.

This sabbat marks the longest day of the year; the height of the sun's power. But it's at this point the Wheel begins to wane and we enter the dark half of the year.

The Goddess is very pregnant, as is our Mother Earth. Her bounty has been planted and fertilized, and now the first fruits, such as strawberries, are ready for harvest.

Many rituals for Litha focus on nurturing new life and crops. However, just like motherhood, fatherhood also comes with responsibilities and obligations, hence our focus not just on the mother but also on her consort.

The sun god is represented by the Oak King at this sabbat. Although at the peak of his power, he accepts his responsibilities of marriage and fatherhood and turns his back on the wild and free life of the green woods, even though he knows that this will ultimately bring about his demise.

He again faces his brother, the Holly King, in battle as he did at Yule. Only this time, it is he who must lose and surrender his crown.

Ritual

In our tradition, we capture the sunlight at the peak of its power in crystals. These hold the energy safe as the light begins to wane, until we can welcome the sun again at Yule.

Find yourself a suitable crystal, ideally clear quartz. You will be charging your crystal with power for protection of the sun's rebirth and to call back the light. If possible, the best time to hold your ceremony is midday.

Create and cast your sacred space as you usually would.

If you're just starting out and have absolutely no idea how to cast a circle or create a sacred space, don't worry; we'll get to it later on. For now, be still, calm, and respectful. Be mindful of the elemental energies surrounding you and the presence of the divine, both within yourself and everything around you. Know that what you are about to do is in its honor.

Allow yourself a moment to let the sun's rays fill you and cast a warm glow. You can certainly feel the God's power in the warm sunlight.

Take your crystal and hold it up into the light. Being mindful not to stare directly into the sun, see the light come through the crystal and hold it until you feel it has absorbed enough of its energies while chanting: "We are one, we are one, with the infinite sun."

Take your crystal and place it into a suitable pouch. Close the pouch and store it somewhere safe until Yule.

Close your sacred space as you usually would.

Helpful Tips
You may like to keep your charged crystal safely in its pouch, on your altar, or in another sacred place. If you have a statue or something similar to represent the God, an ideal place would be at his feet.

Lughnasadh or Loaf-mass
Welsh Name: Gwyl Awst—Feast or Festival of August

Time Marked: First day of fall

Short Meaning: Grain harvest

The Lore
Most commonly known as Lughnasadh, this sabbat takes its name from the Celtic deity, Lugh, and the Irish word, *násad*, meaning assembly—literally "a gathering for Lugh." In Welsh mythology, his

counterpart is Lleu Llaw Gyffes, a name that means "the light one with the skillful hand." Although his story differs somewhat from Lugh, he is also strongly representative of the sun's light.

Also termed Loaf-mass or the Grain Harvest Festival, Lughnasadh is celebrated on or about August 2 in the Northern Hemisphere.

So important were grains to our ancestors' very survival, that a great many traditions and customs developed to celebrate, honor, and ensure an abundant harvest. The first and best of the harvest was offered as a libation to the gods, and the first loaf baked from the harvest was suitably blessed, broken into four pieces, and placed in the four corners of a barn to protect the gathered grains.

Something not too dissimilar to this tradition survives to the modern day in the Jewish faith, where a small portion of dough is set aside as an offering known as taking challah.

In our tradition, we know this sabbat as Gwyl Awst, or the Feast of August. It's interesting to note that the month of August, itself, takes its name from *aurum*, Latin for "gold." Though it was originally named in honor of Roman emperor Augustus Caesar, it's an interesting coincidence that the name also calls to mind a regal time of year, as the fields are resplendent with golden grains.

However, this Sabbat marks the end of the road for the Corn King, John Barleycorne, Green Man, or whatever you like to call him. The spirit of vegetation is sacrificed as the grain is cut…he dies three times in all before being ultimately transformed into an adult beverage.

This harvest festival was the only time Pagans drank red wine or berry juice to symbolize the blood of the fallen lord. Gathering the crops was a symbolic act of the success of the power raised at Beltane.

Although Litha marked the beginning of the sun's wane, it is only at this sabbat that this realization truly sets in as the days are getting shorter, shadows are lengthening, and the leaves on the trees are beginning to look tired. Fall is just around the corner.

Although the busy time of the harvest is before us, our thoughts increasingly look inward. We begin a time of introspection as the Wheel turns toward darkness.

Ritual

In our tradition, we typically make corn dollies and burn them as a sacrifice to the God for his death that brings abundance during the harvest time. While this may be ideal in a group setting, it's entirely possible to celebrate this sabbat in an appropriate and meaningful way as a solitary practitioner.

You may like to honor Lleu Llaw Gyffes, the Celtic deity associated with the sun's light.

You will need a suitable candle to represent Lleu and a loaf of cornbread (ideally one you've made yourself; bake and allow it to cool prior to holding your rite). You may also want to have a bread knife to cut the cornbread, but you can always break it with your fingers.

Place your cornbread and Lleu candle on your altar and cast your circle in the normal way.

Light the candle and say:

Lleu, Lord of the Light, Lord of the Sun, I (we) honor you and your great sacrifice.

Focusing on the light of the candle, say:

May we all know the Ancient Ones.

Cut or break three small pieces of cornbread no more than a bite in size. If you cannot eat it due to dietary restrictions, set it aside for birds or as an offering to the wee folk. If you are working with another person, cut and charge three pieces for them as well.

Hold your power hand (the one you write with), athame, or wand over the first piece and say:

> Oak that grows between two lakes,
> Darkening gently sky and glen,
> Unless I tell a lie,
> From the flowers of Lleu are these.

Eat the first piece.

Hold your power hand, athame, or wand over the second piece, and say:

> Oak that grows in upland ground,
> Rain wets it not, heat burns it not,
> It contained twenty gifts,
> It bears in its branches Lleu of the Skillful Hand.

Eat the second piece.

Hold your power hand, athame, or wand over the third piece, and say:

> Oak that grows beneath the slope.
> Shelter of a fair prince,
> Unless I tell a lie
> Lleu will come to my lap.

Eat the third piece.

Helpful Tips
Think about the cycle of the Wheel; connect to the harvest and the abundance. Think about all you have accomplished and set in motion up to this point. Then focus on the peace and calm of the quiet time that will follow this chaotic period of reaping.

Mabon

Welsh Name: Alban Elfed—Light, White, or Height of Water (or Seeds)

Time Marked: Autumn equinox

Short Meaning: Thanksgiving harvest

The Lore

This sabbat is celebrated on or about September 21, and is most commonly known as Mabon, the autumnal equinox.

The sun is, once again, directly overhead the equator and the days and nights are equal; it is a time of balance.

It is interesting to note that the sun moves into the astrological sign of Libra (represented by the scales) at this time of year. The balance here will give way to the darkness.

The harvest is the main focus now, and we celebrate our abundance with a feast of thanks. However, there is an undertone of sadness as we recognize that the light is fading.

The Goddess begins to mourn her fallen consort, who has gone to the underworld.

We do not mourn, though, for we see the God's message of the seeds of life/rebirth in harvest. Remember that reflected by the sabbat on the opposite side of the Wheel, Ostara or Alban Eilir, is the promise of life renewed.

In Welsh, this Sabbat is known as *Alban Elfed*, "the Height of Seeds." It is the Pagan Thanksgiving. We are joyful and take great pleasure in the abundance of fresh foods but should be mindful to focus on the future (or next year's harvest) and set aside the best of the crops as heirloom seeds.

Be grateful to the ancient ones who have provided for us for so long. Express your thanks and enjoy a feast.

Ritual

In our tradition, we typically hold a Thanksgiving-type feast with all the trimmings. We take the time to enjoy our spiritual family and give thanks for all that we've harvested, magickally or otherwise, throughout the year.

You can do this too, if you have a spiritual group or enjoy cooking. Otherwise, why not make a small meal for yourself?

Create and cast your sacred space as you usually would.

As this sabbat is the third harvest, it is an ideal time to reflect on the sacrifices made for our nourishment and give thanks for that abundance. Pay great attention to the presentation of this meal so that those sacrifices are properly honored.

Before anyone eats, focus your energy in an attitude of gratitude and say the following:

> We give thanks to all those who gave for our sustenance.
> May we never hunger.
> May we never thirst.
> May we always have enough to share.
> So mote it be.

Some of the meal should itself be "sacrificed" and placed out as an offering.

You may also wish to bless some seeds and keep them until it's time to plant at Alban Eilir (Ostara).

You can bless them with the following chant:

Release his spirit,
His spirit in the corn.
Release his spirit,
In these seeds he'll be reborn.

Helpful Tips
This is a time to honor our deities and the spirit world, to be thankful for all we have done this past growing season. Stop for a moment, relax, and enjoy the fruits of your personal harvest, whether it be from toiling in your garden, working at your job, raising your family, or just coping with the hustle and bustle of everyday life.

May your Mabon be memorable, and your heart and spirits be filled to overflowing!

Samhain or Night of the Souls
Welsh Name: Calan Gaeaf—the beginning of winter

Time Marked: First day of winter

Short Meaning: Harvest of the souls

The Lore
For many Wiccans, Samhain is the highest of the holy days. It is most commonly celebrated on or about October 31 and marks the beginning of the Celtic New Year and the start of winter, Calan Gaeaf.

As previously mentioned, the day starts at sunset in the Celtic calendar, hence many festivities start the evening before. In Wales, Nos Galan Gaeaf, or Winter's Eve, is also an Ysbrydnos, a night of spirits.

This night is a magickal moment in time, for the veil between the worlds is at its most thin, and we are closest to the door to the spirit world from which our ancestors pervade.

Calan Gaeaf (Samhain) is the last and most somber of the harvest festivals, as traditionally choices had to be made among the livestock as to which could survive the long winter to give birth to new life near Gwyl Ffraid (Imbolc), or be harvested for their meat.

As the animals were slain, the meat was preserved with one of the only known ways of preserving in those times, salt. This is believed to be one of the reasons we use salt in a ritual, to keep away unwanted spirits and protect the circle.

As the animals were harvested, so were the very last of the crops. In fact, whatever was left out after Samhain was thought to belong to the underworld. It was believed that a pooka (a form of hobgoblin), appearing in the form of a black-cloaked headless horseman, was sent to guard the bounty for the underworld deities and torment anyone who would be fool enough to try and take it.

The veil to the otherworld that leads us to the fairies at Calan Haf (Beltane) now opens us to the sacred world of the ancestors, and you may find yourself among their familiar energies once more.

It is common at this sabbat to invite your ancestors to what is called a "dumb supper," where everyone attending eats silently and a place is set to honor those who have passed. In fact, in times of old, people would put food out on their doorsteps for visiting spirits.

As this night is an ysbrydnos, legend has it that things that go bump in the night are not hard to find. In ancient times, it was believed that should a mortal have to venture out on this evening, it was best to do so in disguise to avoid recognition from unwanted or negative spirits. Some say that this is the true origin of Halloween costumes.[7]

As it is the new year, it is also traditionally a time to renew or rededicate yourself on the path, and perhaps take a magickal name.

You may also find it to be the ideal time for banishing the unwanted or undesirable aspects of your life, as it is the last sabbat of the waning year.

Remember, though, that the focus is not on death but on the renewal of life.

Be thankful for all you have and all that is to come. Especially be thankful to your ancestors, without whom you simply would not be.

Ritual

In our tradition, we typically hold two circles. The first is our ancestors' circle, which is quite somber in nature and made specifically for drawing our ancestors near through their memory. As we recount stories of our departed loved ones, we place flowers into a wreath in their honor. The result is a beautiful floral arrangement, which we hang in the West Gate of our sacred space for our main sabbat ritual.

Our second circle, Calan Gaeaf (Samhain), is a more festive occasion, where we dance, sing, and invite those who have gone before to join us and celebrate the turning of the Wheel.

We have used the wisdom gained from our group circles to develop the following magickal working, ideally suited to the solitary practitioner.

For this ritual, you will need a picture and a frame, a chalice or other suitable drinking vessel, and a fitting drink with which to

---

7. Nicholas Rogers, *Halloween: From Pagan Ritual to Party Night*, (New York: Oxford University Press, 2002).

raise a toast, for you are going to call upon your ancestors during this rite and honor those who have gone before you.

Prior to your ritual, you should place pictures of those whom you wish to join you in the frame. You can use as many or as few as you would like. If you don't have a picture, you can write their name or what you called them in this life on a piece of paper and put that in the frame instead.

You can also place mementos of them on your altar. These may be objects that they have given you, or things they enjoyed during their lives—do whatever feels right to you.

Create and cast your sacred space as you usually would.

Focusing on the west, call upon your guardians, guides, friends, and loved ones from the other side. Invite them to join you in your sacred space for this sabbat.

Remember, at this time of year, the veil between here and the other world is thin, so their presence is easily felt.

Meditate for at least nine minutes in silence and see who or what comes to you.

Allow yourself to be open and receive any messages they may have for you.

Pour some of the drink into your chalice, hold it up, and toast the ancestors:

> To those who have gone before me,
> To those who are still a part of me.

You may stay longer and dance or do whatever you wish with your guest.

Close your sacred space as you usually would.

Helpful Tips

For some, this may be a deeply moving and possibly quite sad experience. It's okay to cry; it's perfectly normal to mourn the loss of a loved one. After all, death is what makes life important. That said, try not to be overcome with grief. Instead, align with the joy and love the departed has brought into your life. Be mindful that you are holding this ritual in honor of your loved ones and inviting their spirit to cross the veil so that you might once again enjoy the warmth and love of their fellowship. Nobody wants to go to a pity party, living or not!

You might also want to consider setting up an ancestor altar in your home, if space permits. The ideal location would be the west corner of a room. You don't need to create an elaborate shrine; a couple of pictures or objects that remind you of them and make you smile are plenty.

Above all, remember that without your ancestors, you would not be. You are quite literally the result of the love of thousands.

Summary

In this chapter, we have discussed the sabbats, the eight spokes of the Wheel of the Year, turning and without beginning or end. We have provided some practical examples you can use in your rites to honor and celebrate the sabbats, but remember that these examples are just a place for you to start. Going forward, feel free to adapt and adjust them to fit your needs.

We certainly covered a lot of ground in this last section, so it might be an opportune time to take a break, stretch your legs, and enjoy a nice cup of tea … perhaps with some chocolate biscuits. But don't dillydally too long, as the journey awaits, and we have a very important date … with the moon!

five

The Esbats

In this chapter we go over the phases of the moon and their significance in magick, rites, and rituals. We look at how these connect to the Wheel of the Year and provide yet more practical examples for you to use in your own work.

The Moon Reflects the Light of the Sun

In the previous chapter, we looked at how the great light of the sun represents the God and explored his eightfold journey around the Wheel of the Year. We once again lift our eyes to the heavens, but this time we gaze upon the Goddess's light, the moon. Steeped in the Mysteries, the Goddess moves gracefully through the night sky and offers us magick and transformation.

The light of the moon is actually a reflection of the sun, and in keeping with her role of divine mirror, her journey is eightfold as well; she is always the sun's partner in the sky.

In astrology, the sun and moon are known as the luminaries (as their light is bright enough to cast a shadow); these great lights offer up energy and a focus for whatever they shine upon, be it the phase or a zodiacal constellation.

Thanks to the work of pioneering astronomers such as Galileo, we've learned that the earth revolves around the sun and is not the center of the universe, like the church once taught. In turn, the moon revolves around Earth.

Our planet takes about three hundred and sixty-five days to complete one trip around the sun—a year—whereas the moon takes just under thirty days to complete a trip around the Earth; a "moonth," or, in modern language, a month. One complete cycle of the moon is known as a lunation.

The eight points that mark the sun's journey around the Wheel of the Year are called "sabbats," whereas the points that mark the moon's journey are termed "esbats." Although the moon's journey can be marked at eight points in the cycle, it's not common to hold an esbat rite for every one of these simply due to time constraints. If you were to honor them all, you'd be holding a ritual every three to four days, which is not entirely practical.

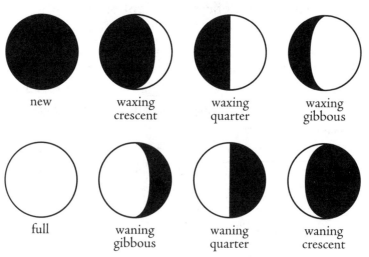

new   waxing   waxing   waxing
                   crescent   quarter   gibbous

full   waning   waning   waning
                   gibbous   quarter   crescent

Accordingly, many Wiccans choose to work only with full moon energies, taking guidance from a line from the Charge of the Goddess: "Whenever you have need of anything, once in a month, and better it be when the moon is full..."[8] However, it is also perfectly clear from this statement that you may do magick as and when the need arises.

Some groups hold rituals at the full moon and teaching circles at the new moon. In our tradition, we add in two more esbats to work with all four of the principal phases: new (crescent), waxing (first quarter), full, and waning (last quarter).

As mentioned earlier, the other four "intermediate" moon phases are very rarely celebrated. Nonetheless, they are quite important in terms of magickal timing, so we'll touch on them a little later.

While on the subject of magickal timing, it's worth mentioning that the energies of each moon phase are considered to be good for up to one day before or after the exact time of that point in the lunation. Obviously, not everyone has the luxury of being able to drop everything and hold a magickal ritual at the precise time (which could well be in the wee hours of the morning), so it's good to know there's some wiggle room. When first starting out, don't get too hung up on the concept of magickal timing. The timing of your work is important, but it's far more important to have pure intent and clear focus.

Let's now take a closer look at the eight phases of the moon's cycle, how they reflect the sun's journey through the Wheel of the Year, and how you can use those energies in your rituals and/or magickal practice.

---

8. Valiente, *The Charge of the Goddess*.

New Moon (Principal Phase)

The new moon marks the start of a lunation and mirrors the sabbat of Alban Arthan (Yule) where the sun is reborn and begins waxing. The moon, which has disappeared from the night sky, is conjunct (an astrological term to mean that two celestial bodies are united, blended, or combined, to work together as one), the sun in the same astrological sign.

From a purely astronomical standpoint, the moon is not actually visible for two reasons: it occupies the same place in the sky as the sun and thus rises with the sun at dawn and sets with the sun at sunset; and as it is in alignment with the sun, none of the moon's surface facing the earth is actually illuminated by the sun's light. Think of it as the moon standing with its back to the sun. If you were somehow able to instantly jump to the surface of the moon and look back, you would see Earth standing full in the night sky.

Something to ponder here is the fact that no matter where we are on earth, we always see the same face of the moon; it never changes. From our perspective, it would appear that the moon does not rotate on its axis as Earth does because you see from where you're standing. However, that is not the case. If the moon were indeed stationary on its axis, it would actually appear to rotate as it orbited the planet, and we would see different parts of the moon. If you're having trouble visualizing this, hold one hand up with your pointer finger straight up and hold your other hand above it with the pointer finger straight down. Holding your first hand still, make a circle around your pointer finger with the other finger. Notice how even though you're not rotating your finger, the parts facing each other are constantly changing.

The moon is tidally locked to the earth, with one rotation on its axis taking about the same time as it takes for the moon to make one complete orbit of the earth, a phenomenon known as synchronous rotation. This means that a lunar day is longer than our twenty-four-hour day here on Earth. In fact, a lunar day is about 29.53 times longer, as its length is equal to that of the synodic period of the lunation (the amount of time between successive recurrences of the same phase).

However, in common with many other religions that tie their rites and rituals to the cycle of the moon, in our tradition we wait to hold our magickal circle until the birth of the new moon, when we can just see the crescent in the sky. The time just prior to this (the three days when the moon is not visible) is known to Witches as the "dark moon," and magick worked during this phase has a very different connotation. Although this is a story for another day and well beyond the scope of this book, suffice it to say that the dark of the moon is a time best suited to clandestine magicks that have a requirement to be worked under cover of darkness to keep them out of sight. Before you hatch a cunning scheme to do just that, you would do well to read the section on ethics in chapter 8 and be aware that you too will be working in the dark. You might want to be mindful of this and wait until you see the crescent of the new moon for yourself before working your magick.

Magickal Energies of the New Moon

Keywords/Qualities: A new start, a time of beginnings, new directions, and options. Initiate new contacts.

Write about what it is you wish to work on or manifest. State your intention and open yourself to the new energies and potential of all that is to come. If you are having trouble getting it down, think about what parts of your life could use a fresh start or benefit from being looked at again in a new light.

This is also a time that offers some new, solid ground on which to build. That said, be mindful: new moon energy can be very energetic and impulsive, making it tricky to navigate. The new moon's energy can also bring emotional confusion, as the moon is so strongly linked to our feelings. Work to be specific in your goals and not get distracted from your true intentions.

Waxing Crescent (Intermediate Phase)

This phase corresponds to the sabbat of Gwyl Ffraid (Imbolc) and marks the beginning of this lunation's spring. The moon has traveled one-eighth (forty-five degrees) of the cycle and a quarter of her face is lit by the sun. At this phase in her cycle, the moon corresponds with the Goddess as Maiden. She rises midway between dawn and midday, and sets midway between sunset and midnight.

It's interesting to note that in the Northern Hemisphere, when this phase occurs close to the actual sabbat of Gwyl Ffraid, the crescent seems to take on the outline of a pregnant belly.

Magickal Energies of the Waxing Crescent

Keywords/Qualities: This is a time for the gestation of the seeds planted at the new moon. Your magickal intention waits, slowly taking root and building strength and clarity.

The crescent phase offers a way to be more deeply connected to the energies available. Your subconscious also holds your intention and begins to get involved, adding energy to your goal. Because of the connection to the hidden strength that is growing, be mindful and specific and hold your intention true. Make special effort not to be distracted and pulled backward into old patterns or karmic energies that may have hindered your work in the past. This is the time of the

Maiden; remember that in the terrestrial sabbats, the Goddess has a strong role to play.

First Quarter (Principal Phase)

This corresponds to the sabbat of Alban Eilir (Ostara), the vernal or spring equinox, where day and night are in balance.

The waxing moon is now midway on her journey from new to full, having traveled one quarter (ninety degrees) of a complete cycle. Her energies are increasing as the crescent is getting bigger.

The sabbat again mirrors the moon's phase, as at this point, half of the moon's face is illuminated by the sun, to bring balance between light and dark. The moon rises at midday and sets at midnight, and thus can often be seen in the afternoon on a clear day.

Magickal Energies of the First Quarter Moon

Keywords/Qualities: The seeds of intention that have taken root and are now being set into action.

The energies of the waxing moon work to grow your plans. Synchronicities begin showing themselves, confirming you are on the right track and helping you hold the vision necessary to attain the goal. If you can see it, you can reach it.

Be strong-willed, keep positive energy flowing, and manage the forces of the growing light. Stay focused, get moving, and make things happen. Nurture and expand.

Waxing Gibbous (Intermediate Phase)

This point of the moon's cycle mirrors the sabbat of Calan Haf (Beltane), the beginning of summer. The moon has now completed three-eighths (135 degrees) of her journey, and the light is growing much stronger with three quarters of her face being lit by the sun. She mirrors the liminal nature of the sabbat by rising midway between midday and sunset, and then setting midway between midnight and dawn; truly this is a between-time. Because of the growing light, the moon is visible in the late afternoon and for most of the night.

Magickal Energies of the Waxing Gibbous Moon

Keywords/Qualities: Passion and deeper connections take hold. With the support of its established roots, the plant now tentatively pokes its stem above the earth and a stalk begins to reach upward.

Now is a time when you may recognize the importance of a good support system and feel the pull to connect with others who can be of service. This is usually a time of meetings and expanded communication, so pay attention to whomever you meet during this phase, as they could be just the person or networker you are seeking to help reach your goal. Many times, success comes from not just what you know, but rather *who* you know.

Full Moon (Principal Phase)

This phase corresponds to the sabbat of Alban Hefin (Litha), the midsummer solstice. The moon mirrors the sun at the peak of his power as her entire face is bathed in his glorious light.

She has completed half of her cycle (180 degrees) and now stands on the other side of the Wheel in the astrological sign directly opposite the sun.

The full moon corresponds with the Goddess as Mother. She rises at sunset, sets at dawn, and dominates the entire night with her magickal and mysterious light. Achieving maximum brightness, she has also reached the peak of her power but now must begin to wane.

Magickal Energies of the Full Moon

Keywords/Qualities: Goals are reached. The Mother Goddess is blossoming in full regalia, standing in full power across the zodiacal sky from her consort. What you had imagined and worked so hard for now becomes reality. This is a time of power, and you can expect results.

The full moon is a great time for any magickal working and many Wiccans use only this time—within the three days of the peak of power—for their spell working. It is considered to be a time of carte blanche, where anything goes. So, do as you will … harming none, of course.

Depending upon when you are able to do your magick, you can work a spell of waxing (increasing or growing) the day before, use the peak of its power for any working on the day of the full moon itself, or work a spell of releasing, using the moon's waning energies, the day after.

Even if you have no need to perform a magickal working, the full moon is also an extremely powerful time to meditate, be thankful, and strengthen your relationship with your deities.

Waning Gibbous (Intermediate Phase)

This point of the moon's cycle mirrors the sabbat of Gwyl Awst (Lughnasadh), the end of summer, and the beginning of autumn. The moon has now completed five-eighths (225 degrees) of her journey, and the light is beginning to fade, although three-quarters of her face are still lit by the sun.

At this phase, the moon rises midway between sunset and midnight and sets midway between dawn and midday. It is visible for most of the night, and because the fading light is still strong, it is also visible in the morning.

Magickal Energies of the Waxing Gibbous Moon
Keywords/Qualities: The key word for this phase of the lunation is validation. Now is also an auspicious time for dreams, so pay attention to them.

At this point, it should be readily apparent whether your plans and actions have come to fruition, or if this is yet another learning experience. It's also a time to share what you have learned or harvested. Use whatever you have manifested to help yourself and others. And if things didn't work out exactly as planned, now is also a really good time to release things that are no longer serving you. However, be mindful to remember the lessons you have learned before you let anything go; in this way, the pain can still result in a "gain" for you.

Last Quarter (Principal Phase)

Sometimes called "third quarter," this phase corresponds to the sabbat of Alban Elfed (Mabon), the autumnal equinox, where day and night are in balance once again.

The waning moon is now halfway between the phases of full and new, having traveled three-quarters (270 degrees) of a complete cycle. Her energies are diminishing as the crescent is getting smaller.

Again, the phase of the moon mirrors the sabbat, as half of the moon's face is illuminated by the sun for a second time, bringing a balance between light and dark.

The moon rises at midnight and sets at midday, so can often be seen in the morning on a clear day.

Magickal Energies of the Last Quarter Moon
Keywords/Qualities: This phase speaks of the importance to find balance in all things. Even though the light of the moon is diminish-

ing, and we now know her demise is inevitable and that she will once again disappear from the night sky, we are reminded that there is life in death, and that Mabon's harvest is not his last breath. While the plants may be dying back and turning to seed, the seeds themselves contain all sorts of amazing potential just waiting to burst into life.

Rethink where you are and where you are headed. Let go of the old, release, and transcend. Push away the things holding you back. Finish up any old business, and clean house. Use this phase of the moon as a magickal harvest, a time of releasing yet remembering, a time to store all you have learned and been working for. Transform, and ready yourself for all that is to come.

Waning Crescent (Intermediate Phase)

This phase corresponds to the sabbat of Calan Gaeaf (Samhain) and marks the beginning of this lunation's winter. The moon has completed seven-eighths (315 degrees) of her cycle; now, only a quarter of her face is lit by the sun. Again, she mirrors the liminal nature of the sabbat by rising midway between midnight and dawn, then setting midway between midday and sunset—once more a time in between.

The phase corresponds with the Goddess as Crone, and, in the same way the crescent mimics the outline of the Maiden Goddess's pregnant belly near the sabbat of Gwyl Ffraid, the waning crescent seems to take on the guise of a boline, or reaping hook. This is especially noticeable when this phase of the moon occurs close to the actual sabbat of Calan Gaeaf, something quite fitting for the last and most somber of the harvests: the harvest of souls.

Magickal Energies of the Last Quarter Moon

Keywords/Qualities: Absolution. The true seed cycle. The seeds always remember their potential. They know exactly what they are to become, but they also understand that they could be compromising their opportunities if they break out too soon— possibly lacking sufficient light to grow, or risking freezing in the coming winter. Patience is key.

Much lies hidden and waiting for you to find it. The energy of the Crone and the occult are at their peak. This crescent represents the Crone's reaping hook, calling the souls and devas back to the otherworld to rest, to remember, and to prepare for all that is to come in the next phase.

Look to the future. The old ends and the new story will soon begin. Be still and make plans, for these are the seeds of intention to be planted at the coming new moon, when the cycle begins anew.

A Circle within a Circle

As the earth circles the sun, constantly turning the Wheel of the Year, so does the moon circle the earth, mirroring the sabbats through the eight lunar phases. We have seen that, just like the sun, we have a spark or first light, with the New moon acting much like Alban Arthan (Yule) and the full moon, fully lit and at its peak of power, much like the sun at Alban Hefin (Litha). Just as the great wheel waxes and wanes, so does the Goddess in the phases of the moon.

A circle within a circle, with no beginning, never ending.

We Are All Touched by the Cycles of the Moon

You learned in chapter 3 that the sun corresponds to the element of fire and the fixed masculine, whereas the moon is associated with the passive feminine element of water.

As the astral body closest to the earth, the moon asserts her authority through the medium of water. Just as she pulls on the oceans to create the tides, she also exerts her influence upon the very water from which we are mostly made. She has a profound effect upon each and every one of us that touches all aspects of our being—physical, mental, and spiritual.

Even though she holds great sway, we are not necessarily aware of her influence upon our lives, for just like the gentle and guiding arms of a devoted mother, her natural, loving embrace has been constantly with us from the moment we were born.

As a representation of the Divine Feminine, it's hardly surprising to find the moon is so strongly connected to the monthly cycle of the female body. Even the word "menstrual" has its etymological root in the early Latin *mensis*, meaning "month" or "moon cycle." In fact, recent scientific research conducted by the Anthropology department of Indiana University has identified a definite tendency for the female reproductive cycle to actually synchronize with the cycle of the moon's phases.[9]

It has long been thought that the moon also influences the water in plants, as well as the soil in which they grow, so the cycle of the moon is significant to those involved in agriculture. Although Roman naturalist Pliny the Elder first wrote about this cycle nearly two thousand years ago, many present-day farmers, gardeners, and horticulturalists plant, prune, reap, and sow by the moon.

The element of water is strongly associated with our emotions and these, in turn, affect our mental state. The influence of the moon can, quite literally, be mind-altering. In less enlightened times, those suffering from mental illness were termed "lunatics," and while we may no longer use this term, any first responder or emergency room nurse you care to ask will tell you that people do some decidedly strange things when the moon is full. Moreover, scientific research

---

9. Amy L. Harris and Virginia J. Vitzthum, "Darwin's Legacy: An Evolutionary View of Women's Reproductive and Sexual Functioning," *The Journal of Sex Research*, vol. 50, (Abingdon, UK: Routledge, 2013), 207–246.

has concluded there is a definite correlation between lunar cycles and human behavior.[10]

But what drives one person mad, may be divine muse for the bard, the spiritual inspiration that causes them to wax lyrical in poem or song.

It's Written in the Stars

Within our tradition we firmly believe that an understanding of astrology is essential for the practicing Witch. We're not suggesting you should become an expert, but your magickal workings will be far more effective if you have even a basic grasp of the subject. The sun and moon, or God and Goddess, perform an amazing astrological dance in the heavens, and offer a vast scope of magickal energies on their way around the zodiac. If you are interested in astrology, it really is quite fascinating.

In common with the theme "you see from where you're standing," astrology is geocentric and looks at the movement of the sun, moon, and planets, in relation to the fixed stars of the heavens, as viewed from the earth.

When our earliest ancestors first gazed up at the night sky, it probably wasn't too long before the more observant of them noticed that sky above their heads was moving. These early astronomers started to recognize patterns in the grouping of certain stars, shapes that resembled animals or other objects, so they gave these constellations names. Incidentally, this act is how astronomers got their name: *astra*, "star" and *noma* ,"name"—literally, "star-namer."

They observed how the stars not only revolved around their heads each night, but that certain constellations also seemed to travel

---

10. Arnold J. Lieber and Jerome Agel, *The Lunar Effect: Biological Tides and Human Emotions* (New York: Dell Publishing Co., 1980).

across the sky over the course of the year; they would disappear below the horizon into the west, only to reappear above the eastern horizon at a later date.

They saw how these movements coincided with the changing seasons and that they always happened at the same time of year. They studied the movements of the sun, moon, and stars so well that they were able to recognize the cycles and patterns of the astral bodies' intricate dance through the heavens. Before too long they were able to look to the heavens and say, with some degree of certainty, when the first snows might fall or when the danger of frost had passed. They had learned to read the language of the stars, and the science of astrology was born.

In fact, astronomy and astrology were the exact same thing until the two disciplines were separated in the eighteenth century. Though astronomy is still considered a science, astrology is no longer regarded as such by the academic community. Nonetheless, the etymology is particularly apt: *astra*, "star" and *logos*, "word" or "study of," to mean literally, "what's written in the stars."

Over the millennia that followed, the precision of measurements improved dramatically, and astrology became a much more exacting discipline, able to determine the likelihood of seemingly unpredictable events with surprising accuracy.

One of the most significant contributions to its accuracy was the adoption of the sexagesimal (base 60) number system, which originated in Sumeria (modern southern Iraq), was passed on to the Babylonians, (keen astrologers themselves), and is still in use today to measure time, angles, and geographic coordinates. Both hours and degrees are divided by sixty minutes, which in turn are divided by sixty seconds. Were it not for the birth of this numerical system, our clocks, calendars, compasses, signposts, and maps would look very different than they do today.

Many of us have a built-in aversion to math, and just the thought of a base 60 numerical system is likely to trigger anxiety. In fact, it's easy, as it's actually programmed into our bodies.

The numbers by which a number can be evenly divided are known as factors, and the number sixty has no less than twelve of them: the numbers 1 through 6, as well as 10, 12, 15, 20, 30, and 60 itself. The large number of factors greatly simplifies things when dealing with fractions. And of all these factors, the most significant are the numbers 5 and 12.

But enough with the scary math, look at your hand. You can easily count to twelve on just one hand by using your thumb to point to each finger bone of your four fingers in turn. Using the thumb and four fingers of the other hand as a tally, you can simply repeat this action five times to get to sixty. Now look at the face of a clock; divided into twelve hours, with each hourly division representing five minutes. Again, we use two hands: the big one to tell the minutes, (12 x 5), and the little one to tell the hours.

Chances are that you actually learned to tell the time long before you had any real mathematical skills to speak of, or indeed any knowledge of the sexagesimal (base 60) number system. But whether you realize it or not, we are inherently attuned to it, for even the optimal resting heart rate of a healthy adult is sixty beats per minute.

Coming back to astrology, it's now easy to see why the Babylonians divided the constantly turning circle of the heavens into twelve parts and identified each of them by their prominent constellations. And just like that, the zodiac was born.

On the journey around the Wheel of the Year, the sun, with the moon in constant chase, moves through all twelve signs of the zodiac, spending about thirty days in each.

In astrology, your sun sign (or natal sun) is the part of the zodiac where the sun is standing at the time of your birth. Think about what sign of the zodiac your sun sign would be if you were to be born this very day.

If the moon is new today, it will be in the exact same zodiac sign as the sun. But if the moon were to be full, it would be in the opposite sign, dancing like a mirror in the night sky, reflecting the full light of the sun onto the earth.

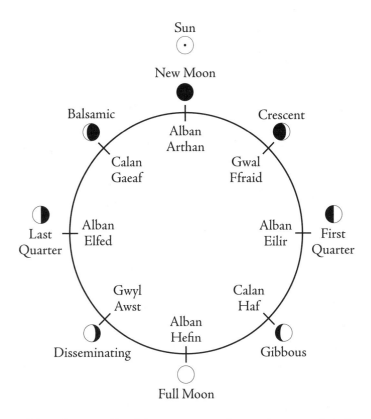

There is a standing joke among astrologers that goes that there aren't actually twelve signs of the zodiac, just six and their reflections. Certainly, when it comes to the relationship between sun and moon, which signs are mirrored across the Wheel of the Year are especially poignant.

For quick reference, here are the signs and their reflections:

Aries—Libra
Taurus—Scorpio
Gemini—Sagittarius
Cancer—Capricorn
Leo—Aquarius
Virgo—Pisces

Astrology is an amazing rabbit hole to fall into; believe us, you could get lost like Alice for many a year trying to sleuth this all out. But for now, keep it simple and try to work your magick on only new and full moons.

Be aware of which zodiac sign the new moon is in when beginning a spell at that time. Try to be mindful that the sun and moon are conjunct, so their energies will readily combine to work together and achieve a common aim.

However, when the moon is full, she stands directly opposite the sun, offering up the energies of the zodiac sign on the other side. The sun shines his great light upon her, fully illuminating her face and amplifying her energies.

Each of the signs of the zodiac has its own unique set of strengths, weaknesses, qualities, and attributes. But as this is not intended to be a book on astrology, we really don't want to get completely lost down a rabbit hole by going too deeply into them here. However, it is important that you know some key facts to be able to make effective use of their energies in your magick, so here's a short list of correspondences for the twelve signs.

Sign	Element	Keywords
Aries	Fire	The pioneer, the self-starter
Taurus	Earth	Grounding, positive financial energy
Gemini	Air	Communication, short-distance travel
Cancer	Water	The home and healing
Leo	Fire	Action, creative forces at work
Virgo	Earth	Attention to detail, working things out
Libra	Air	Brings balance and harmony
Scorpio	Water	Divination and awakening psychic energy
Sagittarius	Fire	Higher thinking, long-distance travel
Capricorn	Earth	Career gains and taking control of situations
Aquarius	Air	Friendships, strengthening bonds and group working
Pisces	Water	Wade through drama, creative skills like writing and music

Moon Phases and Moon Magick

As we said earlier, esbats are most commonly held on the four principal phases of the moon: new, first quarter (waxing), full, and last quarter (waning). Although there are actually eight phases, most Wiccans (or at least those who wish to retain their sanity), would not attempt to follow them all and work magick for each and every one.

It's interesting to note that most Druids would do their working on the sixth day after the new moon, and that a High Magician would pay more attention to the magickal hour than the phase of the moon. But again, those are topics for another day.

A quick recap of the energies available for each of the four principal phases of the moon:

New moon: Plant the seed—set the intention

Waxing: Put down roots—build, increase

Full moon: Blossom—carte blanche

Waning: Return to the seed—release, banish

Combining Lunar and Zodiacal Energies for Greater Effect

We've said that it's a good thing to know the sign the moon is in for your new- or full-moon working in order to make the most of that lunation, and we've taken a very brief look at some of the qualities offered by each sign of the zodiac. Now let's explore how we bring both together to make the most effective use of energies in your magick.

To effectively harness the energies being offered does, however, require a little thought and planning. Just like people, each sign has some things that certain people warm to and others that rub some the wrong way. Furthermore, what delights or frustrates depends entirely on the individuals involved. Diesel fuel works great in a diesel engine, but not so much in a gas motor. It certainly makes things much more efficient when you're using the compatible fuel to get an engine running properly.

We mentioned earlier how the new and full moons of each lunation occur in pairs of opposing signs. Remember, the new moon is in the same zodiac sign as the sun, but the full moon will be in the opposite sign, 180 degrees across the Wheel. However, opposition is not always bad; by no means do the opposing signs simply cancel each other out—they often have highly compatible qualities. Certainly, if you've ever played with magnets, you've seen for yourself how opposites attract and that they can generate quite the force field between them.

It's worth mentioning that the solar year does not line up with the lunar year, as there are twelve months, but closer to twelve and a half lunations. Because of this, the new and full moons are not fixed within their zodiac sign but move by about two weeks each year. So, if you are reading this now and the new moon is toward the beginning of the sign, midway through the year you may notice it shifts to being toward the end of the sign.

You might also have noticed that the dates for each sign can vary by a day or two each year. Sometimes the next sign begins as early as the nineteenth, and sometimes as late as the twenty-fourth.

Rather than get bogged down in the details, we've listed the average start and finish dates for each zodiac sign. For the most part, these dates cover the vast majority of your magickal workings, but if you are planning a ritual very close to the date on which the sign changes, you might want to consult an ephemeris to be completely sure.

When reading through this guide, remember that we're focused upon the signs and their reflections across the Wheel, so the signs are listed in pairs.

Aries New Moon (March 21–April 20)

Element, Energies, and Attributes: Fire—The pioneer and self-starter. Offering up energy to get you motivated, a time to begin a new project.

Practical Magick: Work some candle magick to inspire and kick start your new ideas.

Libra Full Moon (Sun in Aries)
Element, Energies, and Attributes: Air—Balance and harmony. Offering energy to bring justice and peace to a situation. Settling difficulties and calling a truce.

Practical Magick: Use a feather quill pen to write out your desires for peace.

Taurus New Moon (April 21–May 20)
Element, Energies, and Attributes: Earth—Grounding and protection. Set a focus and root an intention.

Practical Magick: Program a hematite crystal for protection to be carried for the next two weeks.

Scorpio Full Moon (Sun in Taurus)
Element, Energies, and Attributes: Water—Awakening psychic abilities. Work with divination, spirit guides, and guardians to see your way forward.

Practical Magick: Try scrying for answers by dripping hot wax into a bowl of water and seeing your messages in the images the wax makes.

Gemini New Moon (May 21–June 20)
Element, Energies, and Attributes: Air—Communication, short-distance travel. Outline written projects, begin to make plans that involve the understanding and cooperation of others.

Practical Magick: Write an enchantment to get things moving in your head. For example: "Money is flowing to me in all good ways."

Sagittarius Full Moon (Sun in Gemini)

Element, Energies, and Attributes: Fire—Higher thinker, long-distance travel. Set vacation plans and safe travel into motion.

Practical Magick: Program a leopard skin agate crystal to use as a safe travel charm.

Cancer New Moon (June 21– July 20)

Element, Energies, and Attributes: Water—The home and healing. Great time for house cleansings.

Practical Magick: Create a holy water using moonstone and ritual salt blended with spring water. Charge it with the Cancerian energy and sprinkle it around your home for clearing.

Capricorn Full Moon (Sun in Cancer)

Element, Energies, and Attributes: Earth—Career and taking control of situations. Use this energy for financial gain, prosperity magick, or finding just the right job for you.

Practical Magick: Use green ink to write out what you wish to manifest. For example: "I am living a joyful and abundant life." Read this every morning at your altar for the next two weeks.

Leo New Moon (July 21–August 20)

Element, Energies, and Attributes: Fire—Action and beauty. Work on your appearance, your confidence, or self-esteem.

Practical Magick: Energize some new clothes, place the energy of confidence in their fibers, and when you wear them, let yourself feel beautiful.

Aquarius Full Moon (Sun in Leo)

Element, Energies, and Attributes: Air—Friendship and group work. This is a great time to circle with friends and offer magick on behalf of others—harming none, of course.

Practical Magick: Invite others to work with you. Each be the battery to charge each other's good wishes.

Virgo New Moon (August 21–September 20)

Element, Energies, and Attributes: Earth—Attention to detail and working things out. This is a good time to start a new diet or fitness program. Use the energy to make solid plans.

Practical Magick: Begin a food or exercise journal. Dedicate it in your circle under this new moon.

Pisces Full Moon (Sun in Virgo)

Element, Energies, and Attributes: Water—Dealing with drama and being creative. Great energy for dealing with the pettiness of others. Also a good time to write poetry or create music.

Practical Magick: Let this full moon's energy be your muse. Open yourself to write a story about the gods which may inspire others not to be so difficult.

Libra New Moon (September 21–October 20)

Element, Energies, and Attributes: Air—Balance and harmony.

Practical Magick: Create a clearing incense or use sage. Cleanse and clear your mind; work to seek a balance within your heart center.

Aries Full Moon (Sun in Libra)
Element, Energies, and Attributes: Fire—Pioneer or self-starter. This moon offers energy to manifest your passions and desires.

Practical Magick: Carve a candle to manifest your desires and burn a little of it each day for the next two weeks.

Scorpio New Moon (October 21–November 20)
Element, Energies, and Attributes: Water—Awakening psychic abilities. The energy allows us to look inward.

Practical Magick: This would be a good time to do more self-exploration and begin to set out a new plan of esoteric study.

Taurus Full Moon (Sun in Scorpio)
Element, Energies, and Attributes: Earth—Beauty and luxury. Good energy is being offered for prosperity or love magick.

Practical Magick: Write your wishes on a small piece of paper and bury them in a potted plant to grow your wishes.

Sagittarius New Moon (November 21–December 20)
Element, Energies, and Attributes: Fire—Higher thinking, long-distance travel. Explore and learn about other cultures. This energy promotes a search for the truth. We can now use some of the knowledge gained to move ourselves along.

Practical Magick: Cast your sacred space and go on a past life meditation. You may find out why you are so interested in places you have never visited in this incarnation.

Gemini Full Moon (Sun in Sagittarius)

Element, Energies, and Attributes: Air—Communication and short-distance travel. Flirtation and inquiring minds that need to know. Communication is a key element of Gemini, and this moon offers great energy to network and get to know people.

Practical Magick: Make a list of the kinds of people you wish to draw into your life. It can be for career or just expanding your social network. Consult a divination tool such as the tarot and ask how you can meet them.

Capricorn New Moon (December 21–January 20)

Element, Energies, and Attributes: Earth—Career and taking control of situations, offering us an energy of accountability. We can rejoice in all that we are and make a plan for the positive changes we intend to bring about.

Practical Magick: Start a savings jar or piggy bank and charge it with this new moon's energy. Start by adding a dollar bill you have anointed with an oil that corresponds to Capricorn or Saturn. Then add funds to it every day and watch it grow until you have reached your goal.

Cancer Full Moon (Sun in Capricorn)

Element, Energies, and Attributes: Water—the home and healing. The perfect energy for spell work to bring about good health.

Practical Magick: Make a healing elixir—charge a glass of spring water with blue lace agate. Add the glass back to your gallon and drink some every day to promote well-being.

Aquarius New Moon (January 21–February 20)

Element, Energies, and Attributes: Air—Friendship and group work. Promotes humanitarianism and giving to others for the betterment of all. A good time to release bad habits and get organized.

Practical Magick: What is it that you have been holding that no longer serves you? Write it out on a piece of paper and burn it in your cauldron during your ritual. See the bad habit leaving by going up in smoke.

Leo Full Moon (Sun in Aquarius)

Element, Energies, and Attributes: Fire—Action and beauty. Known as the barren moon, this is not a time for planting but more of an offering of change, particularly in perspective and appearance—thereby getting noticed.

Practical Magick: Candle magick is a great idea for the Leo full moon spell working. Charge a piece of jewelry in candle light. (Leos love jewelry), and wear it to attract positive people and allow you to be noticed.

Pisces New Moon (February 21–March 20)

Element, Energies, and Attributes: Water—Dealing with drama and being creative. Service to others. Dreams become psychic and we can clear up loose ends.

Practical Magick: Create a dream mojo or pillow. Seek out some herbs which you like the smell of, and that work well with dream time, such as lavender. Add a piece of jade or amethyst and ask for prophetic dreams to come to you. Place the mojo under your pillow and keep a dream journal.

Virgo Full Moon (Sun in Pisces)

Element, Energies, and Attributes: Earth—Attention to detail and working things out. Offering an energy to heal past hurts and clear karmic ties.

Practical Magick: Create a plant familiar. Charge some seeds to plant and keep this plant as a friend, not food. As it grows, feel it working with you to clear the air and offer you healing.

In magick, timing in important. However, if the need is great, any time can become the right time. The universe will listen. Remember the words, "Whenever you have need of anything…"[11]

Let's say someone was very ill in the days leading up to the full moon. We should not do a spell to banish the illness, but instead perform a working to bring an increase of good health.

Similarly, if we have a need to perform a prosperity spell prior to the new moon during the time of waning, then we should look to banish debts instead of trying to increase wealth.

Holding your true intention, you can always adjust your working to match the energy available.

More information on spell work and magickal timing can be found in chapter 8.

Summary

In this chapter we've looked at the mystical and magickal moon as representative of the Goddess or Divine Feminine and explored her connection to water, fertility and the very soil itself. We've seen how her lunar cycle mirrors the journey of the God, or Divine Masculine,

---

11. Valiente, *Charge of the Goddess.*

around the Wheel of the Year, and how the principal and intermediate phases of her cycle reflect the energies of the eight sabbats.

You've learned about the magickal energies that each moon phase offers and touched on the fascinating esoteric science of astrology to explore how these energies are affected by the moon's journey through the zodiac.

Finally, we've shown you how you can effectively combine the available lunar and zodiacal energies by providing some practical examples that you can use within your own magickal workings.

When you first set out on this path, you may not be very familiar with the phases of the moon and unable to determine exactly where we are within the cycle just by looking at the face of the moon, but as you learned in chapter 2, the secret is not to look … but to observe. Don't just glance at the moon, but really study its face. Do this as often as you can, and before long, you'll become familiar with her dance, and able to recognize where she is in her cycle, just by looking.

We've gone over quite a lot in this chapter, so take a break, stretch your legs, and let it all sink in. Go outside, gaze up to the heavens, and ponder the amazing dance that's unfurling above you.

Don't be in a rush; take as much time as you need. Remember, it's about the journey, not the destination.

six

Not Your Dad's Toolbox

In this chapter, we provide an introduction to magickal tools. We describe what they are, what they represent, and how to use them. We show you how to improvise when you don't have the exact tool you need. And finally, we discuss setting up, and caring for, your sacred altar.

Hidden in Plain Sight

To truly understand the importance and magickal uses of the Witch's tools, we need to cast our minds back to the time when the "Old Religion" was still young and look at the origins of Witchcraft itself.

Generally speaking, there was a time when there were no lines drawn between the magickal and the mundane. Just living life was a magickal thing in and of itself. We were much more deeply connected to nature and the cycle of the seasons than we are today. We trod more softly upon the face of our Mother Earth and had respect for all living things. We used what today is called sympathetic magick to turn the Wheel and ensure the fertility of the land and thus, our own survival.

But even back then, there were those who had a much deeper connection to the nature of nature itself. They learned the cycles of the sun and the moon and how to foretell the changing seasons. They studied plants and herbs and learned how to use them to heal. They used their knowledge for the benefit of all and passed it on to younger generations to ensure it would never be lost. And thus, the ancestral practices of Craft of the Wise were born.

For millennia, the wise ones lived in harmony with nature, appreciated and respected by the communities in which they resided.

But then came the rise of the church of Rome, bringing with it a reign of ruthless patriarchy. With the spread of Christianity throughout Europe, the church's power increased to become almost totalitarian, even subjugating the authority of kings and monarchs.

As it continued to grow, the church sought to rout the last vestiges of Paganism and viewed adherents with disdain. Moreover, they saw elder, educated, and wise women as a threat to their authority, whether or not they practiced any form of folk magic.

A Papal bull was issued to establish the Inquisition and authorize the systematic eradication of Witches. The inquisitors spread fear and panic from the pulpit, offering rewards beyond price for those good people who helped identify the evil Witches. For several hundred years, the word "Witchcraft" was demonized and used as a weapon against the population.

So loud and so often was this message told that a mass hysteria spread throughout the land. Irrational fear spawned religious genocide and the Burning Times were upon us. Historians speculate that between 50,000 and 70,000 people were unjustly killed by burning or hanging during the European Witch trials.[12]

Once the edicts were in place and the Witch hunts began, it was no longer safe for those practicing the old ways to be in possession of the very tools they used for their magick. So they were hidden in plain sight as common household items. The kitchen knife became a boline or athame, the chalice a goblet for drinking, the cauldron a pot to cook in, candles for evening light, and salt simply a preserver.

When reading through this chapter, please be mindful that this is merely an introduction and not a definitive listing of every magickal tool in existence.

As you progress down this path you will no doubt encounter many more fascinating bits of kit, and have the desire to acquire at least some of them for yourself.

That said, we will be the first to tell you that you don't actually need any of the tools we discuss in this chapter in order to create real magick. It's entirely possible to perform all your magickal workings with the most powerful tool already in your possession—your mind.

In the absence of everything else, you can do guided meditation, journeywork, or focus and accomplish truly creative visualization.

Having established that you don't actually need anything, you may well be wondering why we've dedicated an entire chapter to the subject of tools. It's true that having the right tool for the job certainly makes it easier; you can certainly use a butter knife as a screwdriver, but things are going to get frustrating really quickly should you encounter a Phillips-head screw.

---

12. Prof. Ronald Hutton, "Counting the Witch Hunt" (unpublished paper, 2010). Summary available at http://www.summerlands.com/crossroads/remembrance /current.htm.

In addition, what exactly constitutes the "right" magickal tool is largely subjective; these kinds of tools are inherently personal in nature. Some will speak to you, others won't. Ultimately, the decision to use any of the tools we describe is yours alone to make, as is whether you should buy them, or actually make your own.

That said, magickal tools are far more than just empty props. For once you have procured, acquired, or made a particular tool, its energy may be combined with that of your own mind, to become an extension of your energetic body and personal power.

Our primary goal within this chapter is not just to list the tools you may need, but to look at the specific job they do in magick with reasoning and logic, and thereby provide an understanding of their energetic qualities and protocols for their handling, storage, and use.

In order to do this, we must first take a look at the three separate magickal arts or traditions that combine to form modern Wicca:

High Magick: Gerald Gardner gleaned this practice from Aleister Crowley.

Druidry: Gardner had a strong interest prior to his initiation in the New Forest Coven.

Witchcraft: The cunning (or knowledge) of the old ways handed down through the generations and practiced by followers of the Old Religion, like "Old Dorothy" Clutterbuck, who initiated Gerald into the Craft.

Looking at it this way, we can see that each branch seems to have special tools and many of these tools cross over to other branches.

It would be safe to say that the Pentacle, as an arcane magickal symbol, would serve the magician, and the wand, as part of a tree, would serve the Druid. For the Witch, it would be a close call between the athame (an extension of the Witch) and the vessel or cauldron (that which contains, giving form to force).

As we go over our list, keep in mind that you will eventually want to have many of these tools for your own personal use. It's not a race, however; you don't need everything at once. Allow yourself the luxury of collecting your tools slowly—don't just buy the first one you see. Wait until you find the tool that truly speaks to you and to which you feel a strong connection.

Many times, folks come into our shop and say they are setting up their altar for the first time and want to buy everything. A discussion ensues about how these items are sacred, not disposable. Once chosen and consecrated, these items become the responsibility of their owner.

We encourage them to purchase a very simple, wooden-handled athame, one that they can carve later on once they understand its true working value.

We hope that as we go over this brief list of working tools, you will begin to see why we say "allow yourself the journey of finding just the right ones for you." We have also included some extra information that should help you to balance the magickal and mundane.

Altar—a designated piece of furniture for magick and prayer

Not all of us have the luxury of space. Please understand that you can set up your altar on a dresser, nightstand, or even your kitchen table. It is not necessary to have it set up permanently. You can keep the items in a drawer or tool box when not in use, and then smudge or cense the surface before putting the tools back out.

A small chest, dresser, or shelf you can refinish would make a great altar. Not only do you get to breathe new life into something that might otherwise have been discarded; it no longer has to serve a mundane purpose.

The importance of the altar within the Craft cannot be over-emphasized, as it is the focal point of your spiritual practice, the place where you honor your gods and work your magick.

Every other tool we discuss is actually used or kept on your altar, each serving a specific purpose to aid you in the magickal arts.

Altar Cloth—the altar covering of choice

You may wish to work with no covering, especially if you have an altar used solely for magick. But, an altar cloth does serve a purpose. You can match the color to the zodiacal timing, like using a fiery red for Leo, or have a design that connects to the sabbat working, like a holly print for Alban Arthan (Yule). And, if you are using your kitchen table, the cloth can act as a barrier of protection for your tools, separating it from the mundane.

Athame—usually a wooden-handled, double-edged blade

This is one of the most-used tools of any Witch. It should never be used to harm. You would use it to focus your energy, drawing with your power hand and feeling the energy transmitted through the handle to the tip of the blade, condensed into a pinpoint of magickal energy as an extension of you. You would use this tool to call the four directions, bless cakes and ale, and perform Chalice and Blade—an act of sympathetic magick, also termed the Great Rite in Token, which we describe later. Some Witches use their blade to carve candles or focus energy into herbs, medicine bags, poppets, or even another Witch. Energetically, the athame belongs to the God and represents the Divine Masculine.

Bell or Chime—used to represent the element of air or ping an energy

The bell is typically placed on the altar in the east, as it signifies the elemental qualities of air. But keep in mind that the Fae (one of the many names used to describe fairies and sylphs, the elemental beings of air) do not always resonate to metal, as it is said they have an aversion to iron, so you might wish to have a feather or small altar broom in which they could take up residence during your circle.

You may use the bell as a signal to focus the attention of yourself and/or others at key points in your rite, such as calling or releasing the quarters.

You may also use your bell for meditation or astral travel. For example, once in a relaxed state, ring the bell or chime. Listen and allow yourself to see how far you can follow the sound out into the ethers.

Besom—the magickal, working broom

We quite often teach a two-hour workshop just on the meaning and working of the Witch's besom, so we'll try to be brief here, and not go completely off the deep end.

Used primarily to clean and clear, almost like you would with smudging feathers, you may sweep the altar or any items you wish to clear of unwanted energy.

The broom or besom has a leading role to play in sympathetic magick and is connected to all four agricultural sabbats. At Gwyl Ffraid (Imbolc), it sweeps Brid's bed to ensure the fertility of crops, whereas at Calan Gaeaf (Samhain), it clears the circle for the arrival of the ancestors.

At Calan Haf (Beltane) it is used to act out the ritual magick of jumping the broomstick, to honor the union of God and Goddess, while at Gwyl Awst (Lughnasadh), the broom sweeps the barley corn from the miller's floor.

There is a wonderful anecdotal story behind why Witches are often depicted flying upon brooms, and we love to demonstrate this in the workshop. (Insert a cackle.) It all has to do with fertility rites. The broom was taken out to the fields and held, skirt outward, in front of the Witch, who would then whack the earth and jump as high as they could with the broom, indicating to the seeds beneath the soil how high the planted crops should grow. To the unknowing, it appeared that the Witch was trying to take off, hence the association with flying. However, most every picture we see of the Witch on a broom shows the handle backward, as the skirt should be in front.

The besom or working broom can also be used for astral travel, but it should *never* be used for mundane cleaning. It should be stored upright, staff to the floor, skirt to the sky, hung in a place of honor or placed on the altar. The broom flower or skirt should never be stored on the floor, for it is a tool of air or flight, not one of grounding.

Boline—white-handled or crescent knife

This sacred knife is used to gather or harvest herbs such as mistletoe. It may also be used to carve candles, particularly by those Witches who would never dream of using their athame to cut or mark anything.

As a representation of the Crone's reaping hook, the boline is also often used in acts of sympathetic magic and during initiation rites. Again, just like the athame, this blade is never used do to harm.

Book of Shadows—the records of magickal working

Records of rituals, spell work, and other magickal works are written in the pages of this book. These might be entirely your own work or may be copied from a mentor if you are part of an initiatory tradition.

There is some confusion as to the difference between a Book of Shadows and a grimoire. Strictly speaking, a Book of Shadows is a record of what went on during a ritual, whereas a grimoire is book of instruction on how to perform magickal workings—a kind of magickal textbook, if you like. The grimoire takes its name from *grammaire*, an Old French word used to describe any book written in Latin. But by the eighteenth century, most French books were published in the native language, save for a few magickal textbooks which continued to be circulated as Latin manuscripts. Eventually this gave rise to the corruption of *grammaire* to *grimoire*, a figure of speech implying that the work was hard to understand and would probably cause you to grimace while trying![13]

To be precise, Gardner's first Book of Shadows, *Ye Bok of Ye Art Magical*, is actually a grimoire as it contains far more in the way of instruction for practitioners of the Craft than records of rituals held. No matter what you term your book, you should, at the very least, have a ritual for each sabbat and new and/or full moon esbat you celebrate. You may also want to include spells you plan to use or have used along with their results.

Bowls—small vessels for salt and water

The ritual salt is mixed into the water and used to asperge (ritually sprinkle) participants, the sword, or other items you wish to cleanse and clear.

In our tradition, we use a pair of matching ceramic bowls with the same design but of different color—blue and brown. We designate the blue one as water and the brown one as salt (earth).

---

13. Owen Davies, *Grimoires: A History of Magic Books*, (New York: Oxford University Press, 2009),.

You don't have to use ceramic bowls, as you could certainly use glass, crystal, or a natural container, like a seashell for the water. Use your imagination and get creative! That said, do try to avoid plastic—it's not very special or sacred.

Candles—used for magick and to light the Watchtowers

Although candles are often found on the Wiccan altar, they do not represent the elements or your deities; instead they are lit to honor them and light their way. We covered this in some detail back in chapter 3. If you're still not clear, we would urge you to go back and take another look.

Candles are most commonly used within a working for healing, prosperity, or love magick.

When selecting candles for your altar, try to avoid cheap and overly-synthetic scented candles. Buy the best ones you can afford, ideally created with specific magickal intent. Better yet, make your own!

Cauldron—the vessel

Belonging to the Goddess or the Divine Feminine, the cauldron is strongly associated with the element of water. However, as you can see by its many and varied uses, it really brings together the four elements of air, fire, water, and earth, and imbues them with the fifth, spirit.

It symbolizes the "Star Goddess, in the dust of whose feet are the hosts of heaven, and whose body encircles the universe."[14] It is the container that holds the raw, undifferentiated potential from which all things proceed and to which they must return. As representative of the Goddess, the cauldron contains within it the energies of

---

14. Valiente, *Charge of the Goddess*.

inspiration, transformation, and regeneration. Within your magickal workings, it can be used to hold a special liquid or brew, to hold sacred earth and seeds, or to mix herbs and salts. You can also use it to safely hold burning candles (as a representation of fire) or incense to make smoke.

Censer—used to burn incense

You can use something as simple as an incense boat or you can go all-out and spring for an elaborate, brass, swinging or handled censer, which burns special handcrafted incense on charcoal. In the same way as the salt/water bowls are used to asperge things to cleanse and clear, the censer is used consecrate and purify things, by censing them in the smoke of the burning incense.

Chalice—the ritual cup

Also belonging to the Goddess or Divine Feminine, the chalice is strongly associated with the element of water.

It is used, along with the athame, in the Chalice and Blade ceremony, an act of sympathetic magick representing the union of Goddess and God from which all life emanates. Sometimes referred to as the Great Rite in token, Chalice and Blade is enacted by the priestess and priest of a working group and is not generally performed by a solitary practitioner.

It is known as the Great Rite in token or in kind as it is symbolic of the act of sexual intercourse. Within some groups and traditions there are certain circumstances where the Great Rite is performed in true between the priestess and priest, who are most likely a couple. This is a consensual sexual union and an act of great reverence.

If working alone, the athame can be placed flat across the cup of the chalice so that its blade and hilt form a Celtic cross, thus representing the union.

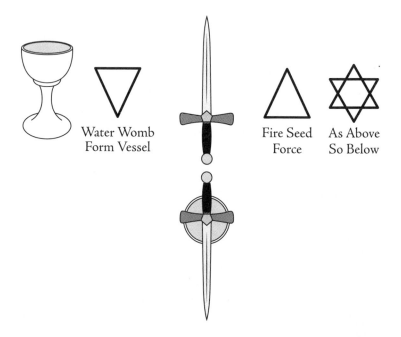

Water Womb   Fire Seed   As Above
Form Vessel   Force   So Below

The chalice often holds the wine or other drink of choice. All may drink of the blessed liquid and some is saved for libation or sacred offering.

Clothing—your Witch-wear

This does not have to be an expensive robe. You can make one quite simply out of a sheet. Keep in mind that it is easier to work magick if you *feel* magickal; wearing a designated "working" outfit or cloak can make you feel like you are indeed covered in magick. Some like to go sky-clad (sans clothing), but you should decide what is best for you and fits the occasion.

Cord—not just for hanging a pouch

Although there are many kinds of cords within the Craft with many different uses, we're going to focus on the cord you would tie around your waist.

Unless you are given one by your High Priestess, this is definitely something you're going to have to make yourself. But how long should you make it?

Many working groups, especially those not part of an initiatory tradition, would consider the cord be a type of measure in kind, and make the cord as long as you are tall. Other groups might have a specific magickal number that the cord must equal, for example 81 inches because it connects to the number nine.

The cord can indeed be used to hold a pouch, but it can also be used for much more. You may use it to form a ring in which to work, or perhaps perform cord magick, by tying and releasing knots. In fact, there are so many ways that cords can be used in magick, we actually teach a two-hour workshop dedicated to just this subject to the "Witchlings" in our tradition.

Crystals—rocks and gemstones

Each of these beautiful gifts from the earth holds a magick of its own. They are wonderful to include in the north corner of your altar, as a fitting place for your earth elementals to reside. As they are so strongly connected to the physical realm of earth, you may also wish to use them in manifestation magick to make your ideas a reality, or program them for healing, stability, and protection.

Divination Tools—the "-mancies" from A to Z

From astromancy (divination from the stars) to zoomancy (divination from the movement of wild animals), and all that lies between, this section on divination tools could span several books. Suffice it to say that any Witch worth their salt should have at least one form of divination in which they are somewhat proficient.

When it comes to tools, the world is your oyster; there are all manner of tarot decks, oracle cards, crystal balls, runes, sticks, and stones readily available to choose from nowadays. Yet as before with ritual tools, you don't really need anything specialized at all; you can effectively scry in a candle flame, mirror, or simple bowl of water to receive your messages. You could even lie on your back and gaze up into the clouds to gain your inspiration.

We all have an intuitive ability, but it takes work and practice to develop it. Think about what speaks to you, be it tarot, astrology, numerology, runes, scrying, or pretty much anything that floats your boat, and start to work with it. Each day, devote some time (no matter how much) to learning and practicing your divinatory art, and you'll be amazed how quickly it becomes familiar. Before long, you'll be able to use you chosen tool to help gain insight and information for any given situation.

Many working groups perform group divination as a form of magick and support for each other, but even a solitary practitioner can benefit from divination as a way to track your progress on the path through the energy of spirit.

Jewelry—adornment for your craft

In days gone by, it was unwise to advertise the fact that one was indeed a Witch; wearing ritual jewelry in public was definitely not done. Many Witches also believed that their magickal powers could be held or stored within their ritual jewelry, which should only adorn their person when they were ready to work the magick.

Today, many of us can wear our jewelry with pride. But do keep in mind that if you are going to wear your magickal items in the mundane world, you also carry with you the responsibility of protecting them and possibly explaining them to some degree.

We encourage our working Witches to wear a pentacle much like a Christian would wear a cross, to keep them connected to the ancient ones and their path. We also equip them with words of wisdom in order to defend it, should the need arise. We certainly do not promote proselytizing, but should they be challenged, they have the knowledge and eloquence to explain its true meaning to someone not of the Craft.

Pentacle/Pentagram—an altar tile

A pentagram is a five-pointed, woven star, whereas a pentacle is a five-pointed, woven star with a circle around it. It's easy to remember pentacle, circle. When used in the context of a magickal tool on your altar, it acts as a shield, a portal, and as place of consecration. Some say it represents the element of earth, but we believe it is connected to all the elements and spirit.

Snuffer—used to extinguish all candles

Some believe that blowing out candles is an insult to the element of fire, yet others believe that wetting your fingers with spit or salted water and pinching out the flame is just as insulting. For this reason, you might want to consider acquiring a candle snuffer so that none can take offense.

Another alternative, if you can (and with a bit of practice) is to simply clap your hands and create energy that allows the flame to disappear ... as if by magick.

Statuary—figures to represent your god and goddess

It's wonderful if you can find a depiction of your deities in statue form to place upon your altar, especially ones that resonate with you and truly speak to the deity or deities' energy. Unfortunately, there are instances in which you won't find a very good likeness. Keep in mind that you could use your favorite picture of the deity in a frame along with an appropriately colored candle to honor their presence. Or you could even use another object altogether that represents that god or goddess; for example, a small set of scales for Anubis or Themis, a shell for Aphrodite, or a sun and a moon to represent the Divine Masculine and Divine Feminine.

Sword—used to cast the circle

Most commonly used in working groups as opposed to solitary practitioners, the priest or priestess uses a ritual sword to circumscribe the perimeter of the magickal circle. While the priest or priestess outlines the circle, the other members visualize a beam of energy emanating from its tip to create a ring of glowing light that forms a protective barrier between the worlds.

As a solitary practitioner and in the absence of a sword, you can always use your athame to cast the circle just as effectively.

Wand—symbol of magick and authority

Holding the energy of the sacred woods, the wand is also an extension of the powers of its wielder. Wands are used not only as a symbol of honor, but also as a tool to control energy when used along with an enchantment or spoken word. Just like the athame, it focuses and directs energy, only in a less demanding yet considerably more alluring way.

Folklore and custom say that the wand is traditionally made of hazel, but you could create your own from any sacred wood with which you have a strong connection. Personalizing your wand in this manner may give it its own unique meaning and magickal qualities.

Once again, we are constrained by the space available to provide only a brief insight into this incredible tool. Nonetheless, we do strongly recommend that you make, procure, or otherwise acquire a wand of your own (similar to the athame); it will become an extension of your energetic body and your ally in the magickal arts, albeit in a far more subtle way.

Summary

Within this chapter we've tried to address the age-old question we're so frequently asked: "What tools do I need to have in order to be a Witch?" First, and foremost, you need your mind; it provides a clarity of the work at hand and is the singularly most powerful tool in your possession. Everything else is secondary.

Again, it's not necessary to acquire everything as fast as you can in order to be an effective Witch—it's not a race! Be mindful of your budget and learn how to adapt and improvise.

That said, magickal tools are great to own and can certainly assist in the efficiency and effectiveness of your magickal workings. But please, please keep in mind, if you are going to own it and work with it, you are responsible for it. Use them, store them, and care for them with respect, for they are an extension of you. And, above all, when the time comes to part company with them, perhaps because they are worn out, broken, or damaged, dispose of them with the ultimate of respect and gratitude for the service they have given you.

Many folks ask us what tool they should acquire first, and then having obtained it, what to get next, and so on.

To provide some guidance on this, the following list is ordered in terms of importance:

1. An athame or wand for wielding your power

2. The altar for a sacred place dedicated to do your work

3. A representation of your god and goddess

4. A representation of the four elements

5. A chalice or cauldron—a sacred vessel to contain your magickal workings

6. A cord to create a sacred space in which to work your magick (or hang your pouch)

7. A pentacle—the sacred symbol of the Witch

8. Jewelry and ritual wear (… or not, if you want to go sky-clad)

9. (Optional) A divination tool to gain knowledge or information

As said earlier, this is far from an exhaustive list of all the magickal tools you will encounter. One thing's for sure, though—you're not likely to find them in your dad's toolbox … unless he's a Witch too!

seven

In the Name of the Gods!

Here we look at the process of choosing a pantheon and deciding upon which gods and goddesses to honor. We talk about the importance of having compatible deities so they will not detract from the energies of your circle. And finally, we discuss the power of words and how they affect your choice of a magickal name.

Deciding upon a Pantheon

We should probably begin by defining the term "pantheon," a word that, perhaps unsurprisingly, also has Greek roots. derived from *pan*, "all," and *theion*, "holy," itself from *theos*, "god" to mean "all holy (or holies). Originally, *pantheon* was the name of a circular temple in Rome built by Marcus Agrippa around 25 BCE where all the gods were worshiped. In more recent times, the word has come to mean a collection of deities ("all the holies") belonging to a particular culture.

What pantheon you choose is a matter of what you feel drawn to. If you have some ancestral connection to a particular culture and it's within your roots, that's great but is by no means necessary. The fact that those culture's deities speak to you is all the justification you need.

Wiccans traditionally choose from Celtic, Egyptian, Norse, or Greek pantheons. More modern Wiccans have expanded their choices to include East Asian, Roman, West African, and even Christian deities (e.g., saints and angels).

A Personal Connection Is Essential

One of the first things we tell folks who are seeking kinship with a deity is to find a personal connection with your pantheon. As mentioned earlier, it could be in your blood and you have a genetic link to that culture. It might also be one of your past lives. Or maybe it's a deep spiritual connection that truly resonates with you and you can't really explain. Perhaps one day you were reading through some material and it triggered a kind of déjà vu; the story you were delving through seemed strangely familiar and you got all sorts of confirmation chills just from reading it.

Whatever brings about your personal connection is fine, but don't attempt to build a relationship with a deity without a personal connection to the culture. We strongly counsel against making a random, hurried, or otherwise ill-considered choice, such as, "Ooh, Hecate seems cool … I'll start there," or you may find you have cause for regret when she tests your knowledge and sincerity.

Deciding on Your Personal Deities

Many of the revealed religions, especially the Abrahamic ones, state that there is but one god and that all else comes from that single male source. Research in comparative religions, however, would seem to indicate that most every other religion features a Great Mother figure within their theology. Even Christians allowed for reverence of Mary and Saint Brid or Brigit.

In Wicca, we most commonly honor both the Divine Masculine and the Divine Feminine: the God and the Goddess from which all life comes. After all, how can life be created without a womb for gestation?

There are other branches within Wicca, such as Dianic, that honor only the Goddess, but covering them is beyond our scope here.

Fortunately, within the Craft we have whole families of gods and goddesses from which to choose, and almost every pantheon offers a strong Masculine/Feminine balance, and some even have gender-fluid gods.

Are Your Deities Compatible?

Having determined that you're going to need both a god and a goddess, there is another important question you need to ask: Will they work together or against each other? This really is something you should consider if you are aiming for effective magickal workings.

Our advice on this subject is short and simple: Don't mix and match your pantheons. We fully understand that this may ruffle the feathers of some eclectic Wiccans out there who ardently believe one of the most attractive qualities of Wicca is the freedom to do as you please, but we've seen the chaotic effect that unsuited deities can have on a circle firsthand on more than one occasion.

Even if you've done a boatload of research and can see how the mythology of a particular god from one pantheon seems to parallel the story of a goddess from another, it is not wise to try and mix their energies. Our experience has shown us in no uncertain terms that they work best within their specific families and tend to gravitate toward their own partners.

Consider the following example, where we examine the thought processes of an imaginary neophyte deciding upon which deities to honor:

"I love Thor—he's a kick-ass god! I know him well and he always helps me, though he demands a sacrifice for his aid. I also heard about Quan Yin, and after doing some reading, discovered that she made some serious sacrifices to bring healing to the world. I really need healing in my life, so how about I put the two of them on my altar together?" What on earth makes you think they want to be married up?! Wouldn't it better to work with a goddess from within Thor's own pantheon? In this case, you could call on his wife, Sif, a Norse goddess of compassion and fertility. He will be familiar with what she expects of him, and hopefully, you'll already have a relationship with his family.

That's not to say that if you feel especially drawn to Quan Yin, you couldn't work with her for a specific rite and get to know her. Perhaps it would be best in this case to make some sort of offering to her in anticipation or return for the healing work she performs on your behalf.

But *please* don't put them both on your altar and try and work with them at the same time. Their energies are about as conducive as a surfboard in the Sahara. Sand dunes might be formed by the wind, just like waves. But you sure can't hang ten and ride them in the same way.

Know Your Pantheon and Know It Well

In order to get the most out of your magickal workings, you need to foster a strong working relationship with your chosen deities.

Just like us mere mortals, the gods and goddesses have their own set of likes, dislikes, peculiarities, foibles, and different ways of getting things done that you would do well to learn. Unlike us mere mortals, who are here and gone in the blink of an eye, the gods and goddesses have been around for a very long time. They are, unsurprisingly somewhat set in their ways.

Do not expect that they will make allowances for you and adapt to your expectations—it isn't going to happen. It is *you* who must adapt to fit in with the deities of your chosen pantheon by devoting yourself to learning their ways and aligning with the energy they have to offer.

It might help to think of it as though you are going to live with a spiritual family in their spiritual home (the place you go every time you cast a circle). You don't own the place and are only a guest, so you'd better know what you are getting into.

Be gracious. Take the time to learn about your hosts and what you can expect of them and, perhaps more importantly, what they expect of you. As you progress along the path, the nature of your relationship with your deities becomes increasingly intimate. To illustrate, let's continue with the analogy.

When first starting out, it's very much as though you're just passing through, like you've just graduated high school and are taking a gap year to backpack across Europe before starting college. You want to experience the sights, sounds, and energies of a multitude of different cultures but still need to be mindful of all these places' customs and laws so you won't end up in trouble many miles from home.

Dedicating yourself is like starting college and saying you will be a deity's roommate in their house for a year and a day. You will live with that family and abide by their house rules. Sometimes this arrangement is great, and you fit right in. Other times you may feel like a naïve foreign exchange student who doesn't really speak the language or understand the nuances of the culture. Even so, you're only dedicated for a year and a day. Once you get to the end of the college year, you can always move out and make another choice, hopefully more in tune with that which is calling you.

After initiation, things become much more serious. Initiation is not for a year and a day—it is for life. Once a Witch, you are forever seen as a Witch by that family and those of the tradition in which you were raised. Some would say that it's akin to getting married, but we think it goes even further than that: You swear an oath to not only your brothers and sisters of the Craft, but, more importantly, to the Lord and Lady. Your oath binds you even if you should divorce your family. Going forward, your life will reflect how you conduct yourself, especially with regard to the oath you have sworn. Even if you have a huge falling out with your siblings (which does sometimes happen), you are still a Witch and a child of the God and Goddess, a role that comes with responsibilities. In the Craft of the Wise, we learn that we are ever free to choose but never free of the consequences of our choices. It is therefore most important to remain close to the ancient ones and always uphold their ways.

Tips for Building a Strong Relationship with Your Deities

Be a good friend—don't just call when you need something. If you only saw someone who called themselves a friend when they needed you to spot them twenty bucks or a ride somewhere, or help working out their problems, you would probably come to the conclusion quite quickly that they weren't really your friend, and you were actually being scammed or used.

To build a magickal working relationship, you need to be a good friend. And to be that, you need to do all the things good friends do. Call on them to visit, not just to ask for something. Go on astral adventures and visit their homes. Find out all you can about their culture, their language, their heroic feats, and their sacrifices. Get out of your head and into theirs.

Sit and listen to your deities, read about their teachings and family dynamics, and get to know them and all the amazing things they have done. Know their stories, and when you speak of them, speak from your heart with love and respect. Be proud to stand by them, and they will be more inclined to be at your side and take part in your magickal workings.

Make a daily offering—be a devotee. Be thankful for all you have been given already: a warm home, food, and anything you feel is made better by knowing your spiritual family.

Be in service—help others. While the Craft certainly does not proselytize, you can still do good work in the name of your spiritual family, even if you don't seek accolades and recognition in return. Honor and respect are nice, but remember that the knight never stands so tall as when he kneels to help a child.

Basic Advice on Connecting to a Pantheon

We harped on a fair bit about how it's essential to have a personal connection to a pantheon that really speaks to you, and to not just select some deities at random. But what if you're really just starting out and have absolutely no idea what speaks to you? Well, first off, don't fret—everybody's story starts somewhere.

Secondly, cast your mind back to the analogy we gave a little earlier. You have the luxury of a gap year where you can go out into the world and explore. You don't have to decide right away.

Go visit different cultures and learn their stories. Dip your toes in the water of their mythology and search for what feels right.

If you're completely lost and don't even know where to begin your journey of exploration, you can always fall back on the elements.

Here's a look at elemental qualities as they relate to deities, along with a few gods and goddesses who correspond to that element.

> *Air*: Deities associated with learning, meditating, and positive energy. The great "thinker" types such as Cerridwen, Hermes, and Lugh.
>
> *Fire*: Deities associated with kicking butt, projecting, stimulating, and driving forward. Examples are: Aranrhod (Arianrhod), Aradia, Thor, and Mars.
>
> *Water*: Deities associated with healing, poetry, romance, and love. Examples include Venus, Brid, Branwen, and Mannan.
>
> *Earth*: Deities associated with the qualities of focusing, grounding, and growing. For example, Hecate, Isis, Demeter, Don, and Cernunnos.

Using the elements as your guide, put on your backpack and go explore the myriad of cultures that await you. Listen to their stories and discover what speaks to your soul.

If you're not sure how best to actually listen to your deities, we'll just relay the very same Zen wisdom Doreen Valiente frequently used to impart upon her own "Witchlings": "Prayer is asking—meditation is listening." So be still, go within, and listen. When you've found your home, you'll know.

Choosing a Magickal Name

Getting to know your pantheon or family is only half of the job. In order for you to establish a close working relationship with your deities, they also need to know *you*, and how to recognize and identify you. We don't mean the mundane you, the John or Jane Doe embroiled in the drudgery of secular routine, but rather the spiritual you who treads between the worlds. For them to know the spiritual you requires a magickal name. We fully understand that subject of magickal names is in and of itself highly subjective. No doubt there will be others who hold differing opinions, but we happen to believe that names are much more important than many realize. For one, they carry great power as they wield both authority and authenticity. This idea is made quite clear by the first *tynged* or destiny Aranrhod places upon her son in the Fourth Branch of the Mabinogi: "He shall have no name, unless I give it to him."

Lisa has been on the path since 1989, and her first magickal name was chosen for her by her priestess. However, it never really fit her well, and after she'd fulfilled the commitment to which she was dedicated, she went on to choose a name that came to her in meditation. It's also the same name she has used in public gatherings ever since: Binah.

The reasons she felt drawn to take on this name are quite involved, but to be brief, it has a connection to her ruling planet, Saturn, and the understanding of understanding itself. At the time she was immersed in astrology, the chakras, and working the pathways on the Qabalah's Tree of Life. It may not have a Celtic tone, but it is a sphere upon the tree, and trees have a huge role to play in Celtic mythology. However, the most important thing is that the name fits her really well.

When it comes to finding a name for yourself, our advice would be to focus on something in which you want to immerse yourself and choose a name that aligns with that work. That with which you identify identifies you in turn. Have you ever noticed that even pets grow into the name they're given? Or, perhaps, has a pet ever gotten you to name them for the qualities they possessed?

If your group has a High Priestess, she may well give you a name to work under. Hopefully she has earned the right to be raising Witches and will assign you a name that works for you and fits.

Hopefully that name will allow you to take your part in her coven family, as well as the pantheon they follow.

But if you are dedicating in a group that doesn't assign names or you are working as a solitary practitioner, you will need to work at choosing a name that best fits the work you wish to accomplish and serves your highest good.

Understand that whatever name you may choose sends out a signal to the ancient ones and all energies that surround you magickly that *this* is the identity you wish to draw to you. This is how you shall be known. It is part of you, and you are part of it.

Don't be in a rush to come up with something, anything. There is no room for vague ambiguity or haste here. This is your personal magickal identity; you need to really connect with it. Take your time, meditate, and ask your god or goddess to show you or call you by the name.

At the risk of ruffling some feathers, we would also strongly suggest that naming yourself after a god or goddess might not be the best idea. Lisa has been on the path nearly thirty years and knows Cerridwen is by her side and works through her in ritual, but she would never presume to call herself Cerridwen. Although she adores Cerridwen and very much wants to learn all that she wishes to teach her, taking Cerridwen's name for her own somehow smacks of identity theft and misappropriation. It's a bit like calling yourself a crone or sage long before you have done any of the *work* to earn such a title.

How, then, do you find a name? Look to the language and mythology of the pantheon you are working with. Then translate the energy you want into that language.

In times gone by, we were all named after our Craft or our family's responsibility. The barrel maker was Cooper, those at the forge were named Smith, and those who fashioned roofs out of straw, Thatcher. Continuing this today, your electrician might be nicknamed Sparky!

Let's say you are a woman. Think about the esoteric sciences, and what calls to you and drives you to become an adept in the field. Is it crystals, herbs, astrology? Is there an element you want to align with for its energy—air and inspiration, fire and passion, water and intuition, or earth and protection?

We're not suggesting you call yourself "Pixie Flame Moon Quartz"; although it's very descriptive and evocative, we're trying to convey a deeper message.

Let's say you also align with Isis and are beginning work with an Egyptian pantheon. You may want to learn all you can about the Library of Alexandria and all the incredible works that were once housed there, perhaps holding the keys to the Mysteries. Certainly, you'll want to understand Isis and her work with life, death, and rebirth, and you are no doubt learning about others in her family: Hathor, Ma'at, Nuit. But what name should you take? Again, look to the language and history. It might not be too strange to call yourself Rosetta, as this could bring in the understanding of decoding ancient hieroglyphs (themselves keys to the Mysteries), while incorporating the energy of rose, a beautiful color, scent, crystal, and so on. All their meanings combine to assist you on your journey.

Let's say you are a man and identify with the Greek pantheon and are very much into learning all you can about astrology. Rather than call yourself Zeus, the king of gods and ruler of the heavens, you might want to consider translating a name such as "Star Seeker" into Greek. You will find it becomes something like *Anazítisi Asterioú*.[15] Now all you have to do is make sure you are pronouncing it correctly to be able to draw in that energy and the understanding you seek.

---

15. Sources: https://translate.google.com and http://www.systranet.com
   /translate/.

Some people also like to work out the numerology for their magickal name and even play around with the letters, perhaps substituting a Y for an I to get the number with which they wish to align. However, if you have no knowledge or interest in numerology, it's not really relevant at this stage. It's far more important to find a name that calls to an energy, family, or understanding with which you wish to work.

Summary

In this chapter we've looked at choosing a pantheon and emphasized the importance of having a personal connection with your chosen deities. We spoke about how it takes a commitment of both time and work in order to develop this connection, but you should be mindful that if nothing is ventured, nothing can be gained. You could absolutely pull your pantheon out of thin air and put a rubber snake and a Pez dispenser on your altar as deities, but don't be surprised if your circle falls flat on its face owing to a complete lack of cohesive energy.

Finally, we discussed the contentious subject of taking a magickal name and how it is the manner in which your gods can identify you, not something that should be taken lightly.

Realistically, it may take some time, and considerable work, before you are ready to move on to the next leg of your journey and dedicate yourself. But remember, it's not a race. Take all the time you need.

eight

A Place Between
the Worlds

In this chapter, we look at the process of casting a ritual circle: that place between the worlds where we commune with our gods and where magick abounds. We discuss the different types of ritual and detail the steps necessary to cast and uncast a sacred circle. Finally, we again consider the importance of harnessing the available astrological and elemental energies to enhance the effectiveness of your magick.

Although magickal circles can take on many guises generally within the Craft and certainly within our own tradition, there really are just two different kinds of ritual:

+ Sabbat working: Honoring the Wheel of the Year, performing sympathetic magick, mythic role playing, and celebrating the season.

+ Esbat working: Honoring the cycles of the moon, performing magick, initiation rites, or other rites of passage.

The primary distinction is that practical magick is not normally worked at a sabbat, as this is a time to simply celebrate and honor our deities. Unless there is a pressing emergency, initiations, rites of passage, and general practical magick are best accomplished at the appropriate lunar phase (esbat). Should an esbat conflict with a sabbat—for example a full moon on Calan Haf (Beltane)—then the sabbat takes precedence, although it's quite likely that the available energies at this sabbat will be considerably enhanced by the power of the full moon.

Whether you're holding a sabbat or esbat, both rituals also provide ideal opportunities to build stronger connections with your deities.

A Circle Is a Sacred Space

You should always be mindful of the sanctity of the magickal circle and treat it with appropriate reverence. Casting a circle is one of the most sacred acts of magick performed by a practitioner of the Craft. It is a place between worlds, in a time without time, to which you invite your most honored guests; the mundane has no place here.

Never cast a circle without reason; to do so would be inherently disrespectful to the elementals, deities, and spiritual energies summoned to join you. That's not to say your reasons for casting a circle need to be grandiose in their design; it's perfectly okay if all you need is a safe and sacred space in which to meditate and connect with deity. Above all, please be responsible. Don't just cast a circle for "poops and giggles"—it's never a good idea to antagonize the gods!

You can certainly offer a prayer of gratitude, pull a card for inspiration, or even make a daily offering at your sacred altar without the need to cast a circle. It's not necessary to cast for every occasion. But be mindful that if you are working any kind of practical magick, such as burning a candle, you should cast a circle for the safety and efficacy of your work. All acts of magick, intentional or sympathetic, should be performed within the sacred protection of a cast circle. As a circle is the place between worlds, what happens there affects all the worlds.

The Process of Casting a Circle

Let's take a look at how we actually go about creating a place between the worlds, what kind of work we might perform within it, and when we're done, returning it all to the mundane.

As with anything, there are a number of steps to the process and the order in which they are performed is important. Think about making a cup of tea; you can't boil the water until you've filled the kettle.

Steps:

1. The Order of Business

2. Consecration: As Above, So Below

3. Calling the Quarters

4. Casting the Circle

5. Invoking the Goddess

6. Invoking the God

7. Chalice and Blade

8. The Working Itself: Turning the Wheel, or Practical Magick

9. Cakes and Ale/Grounding (optional)

10. Releasing the God

11. Releasing the Goddess

12. Releasing the Quarters

13. Return to the Mundane

So, let's have a closer look at each of these steps: what they stand for, what's involved, and how we go about doing them.

1: The Order of Business

Declare your intention. Say it out loud. It helps to have a specific idea of the work you wish to achieve in the sacred space. Speaking your intention can help you to be mindful to stick with the program, especially if you are working with others. If everyone talks about mundane things, like what they had for dinner, or the last movie they saw during the time you are trying to focus, it may dissipate the energy you have worked so hard to raise.

2: Consecration: As Above, So Below

Once everyone is seated and introduced, the participants should be cleansed and cleared of any mundane detritus they may have brought with them. Cleansing and consecrating acts as a direct, subliminal signal to release the stresses and strains of the day and be ready to focus on the magick at hand.

In our experience, the best way of doing this is to use the four elements: air, fire, water, and earth.

If you have a male and female working partnership, the male can go around the circle and cense people with the smoke of burning incense or a sage smudge stick, combining air and fire. Next, the female would go around and asperge everyone with salted water, thereby combining water and earth. This way you've covered all the bases by using all four of the elements.

If you don't have a partner and are working as the leader by yourself, you could certainly go around twice, or even have the participants cleanse and clear themselves, by passing around the incense and water bowl. Be creative and adapt as necessary, but just be mindful to clear the heart, the mind, and the hands that work the magick.

3: Calling the Quarters

We now set about creating our space between the worlds. To begin the process, turn to face east and call to the direction. Be mindful that you are calling the element, the elementals, and the guardian of the watchtower, so try to craft the words of your call to include them all.

We've included our tradition's invocations a little later on in this section, and you're most welcome to use them as an example. Whatever format you choose for your calls, make sure that they are consistent for each quarter, using words that work to call upon the energies of each specific direction, and end the call with the phrase, "so mote it be."

You can call all four directions yourself, or if working in a group, could have a different person call each of the directions. We would strongly suggest that you don't simply let people wing it but instead put in some prior planning and preparation to ensure the calls are very similar, only changing things that pertain specifically to the particular element being called. Trust us, you do not want to insult a direction by having a bardic poet call to one with an elaborate invitation, only to be followed by someone who is not particularly talented or invested say: "Hey, earth, come be here now." It's important to have congruent energies in order to create a well-balanced circle.

If you are not quite comfortable with writing your own calls, you could certainly work with something like our CD album, *Circle in a Box*. The calls are easy to follow, and you could have a different person hold space for each element called. Or, if you want to take a more active role in the process, you can use the calls we use in our tradition:

All Hail to the Guardians of the Eastern Watchtower
Air, bring forth your elemental power
Guardians of the Eastern Sphere,
we seek your presence here[16]
Come, East, come—So Mote It Be

All Hail to the Guardians of the Southern Watchtower
Fire, bring forth your elemental power
Guardians of the Southern Sphere,
we seek your presence here
Come, South, come—So Mote It Be

All Hail to the Guardians of the Western Watchtower
Water, bring forth your elemental power
Guardians of the Western Sphere,
we seek your presence here
Come, West, come—So Mote It Be

All Hail to the Guardians of the Northern Watchtower
Earth, bring forth your elemental power
Guardians of the Northern Sphere,
we seek your presence here
Come, North, come—So Mote It Be

Starting in the east, turn to face each direction when inviting the energy and light the Watchtower candle to guide them in. Pause for a moment between each call so you truly get a sense of the elemental energies arriving.

---

16. This part of our call was heavily influenced by "A Spring Ritual from 1992," Mary Kay Simms, *The Witch's Circle: Rituals and Craft of the Cosmic Muse* (St. Paul, MN: Llewellyn Worldwide, 1996).

Be sure to close your circle after calling the last direction, by turning again to face east and offering a nod, bow, or other silent recognition.

4: Casting the Circle

If you are working in a group, you should cast your circle in the traditional manner, hand-to-hand. To do this, participants position their hands so thumbs are facing left. This causes the left palm to be facing up and the right palm to be facing down.

The circle is cast in a deosil (clockwise) manner; each person addresses the one to their left. The individual who begins the cast is normally directly to the left of the group's leader. They offer their left hand, palm facing up to the person on their left. Making eye contact with them, they say, "I cast this circle hand-to-hand." The next person places their right hand, palm down, over the offered hand and, lowering their arm to join hands, feels the energy pass. This is then repeated by each person in turn, continuing around until it comes full circle to the group's leader, who makes the final link and declares the circle cast.

If you're working alone, you can't really cast a circle hand to hand, so you might want to use your athame, a cord, or ritual salt (provided it's safe for animals) to designate a ring around your working area instead.

You now have a suitable place in which to invite the old gods. We are aware of certain groups who call the God and Goddess before casting the circle. However, we don't really feel comfortable with this, as we would not invite people to come over if our home wasn't fit to receive guests. And of all the visitors you are ever likely to welcome, the Lord and Lady are surely the most honored of guests. We would suggest it is better to build your place between the worlds before you invite them, rather than expect them to hang around while you construct a suitable abode.

5: Invoking the Goddess

This is usually done by the person acting as priestess. Once received, the person is the go-between, meaning they represent the Goddess to the group and the group to the Goddess.

If you're working by yourself, you should still call the energies of the Goddess into your sacred space. Your invocation could be silent and private or spoken out loud, whichever you prefer.

In our tradition we often read the Charge of the Goddess as part of our invocation:

> Now listen to the words of the Great Mother, who was of old also called among men Artemis, Astarte, Athene, Dione, Melusine, Aphrodite, Cerridwen, Dana, Arianrhod, Isis, Bride, and by many other names.

> Whenever ye have need of anything, once in the month, and better it be when the moon is full, then shall ye assemble in some secret place, and adore the spirit of me, who am Queen of all Witcheries.

> There shall ye assemble, ye who are fain to learn all sorcery, yet have not won its deepest secrets; to these will I teach things that are as yet unknown.

> And ye shall be free from slavery; and as a sign that ye be really free, ye shall be naked in your rites; and ye shall dance, sing, feast, make music and love, all in my

praise. For mine is the ecstasy of the spirit, and mine also is joy on earth; for my Law is Love unto all Beings.

Keep pure your highest ideal; strive ever toward it, let naught stop you or turn you aside.

For mine is the secret door which opens upon the Land of Youth, and mine is the Cup of Wine of Life, and the Cauldron of Cerridwen, which is the Holy Grail of immortality.

I am the gracious Goddess, who gives the gift of joy unto the heart. Upon earth, I give the knowledge of the spirit eternal; and beyond death, I give peace, and freedom, and reunion with those who have gone before.

Nor do I demand sacrifice; for behold, I am the Mother of all living, and my love is poured out upon the earth.

Hear ye the words of the Star Goddess; she in the dust of whose feet are the hosts of heaven, whose body encircleth the universe.

I, who am the beauty of the green earth, and the white moon among the stars, and the Mysteries of the waters, and the heart's desire, call unto thy soul. Arise and come unto me.

For I am the Soul of Nature who giveth life to the universe. From me all things proceed, and unto me all things return. And before my face, beloved of gods and mortals, thine innermost divine self shall be unfolded in the rapture of infinite joy.

Let my worship be in the heart that rejoiceth, for behold; all acts of love and pleasure are my rituals. And therefore, let there be beauty and strength, power and compassion, honor and humility, mirth and reverence within you.

And thou who thinkest to seek for me, know thy seeking and yearning shall avail thee not, unless thou knoweth this Mystery: For if that which thou seekest, thou findest not within thee, thou wilt never find it without thee.

For behold, I have been with thee from the beginning, and I am that which is attained at the end of desire.[17]

6: Invoking the God

This is usually done by the person acting as priest. As with the Goddess, the person becomes the go-between. Once received, they represent the God to the group and the group to the God.

Again, if you're working by yourself, you should still call the energies of the God into your sacred space. As before, your invocation could be silent and private or spoken out loud, whichever you prefer.

Within our tradition we also often read the Charge of the God, a poem heavily influenced by and very much in the style of Doreen's Charge of the Goddess. Although its origins are unknown, it makes a fitting partner to the Charge of the Goddess in ritual. There are

---

17. Valiente, *Charge of the Goddess*.

several versions in existence, but the one we use in our rituals we largely rewrote ourselves to suit our tradition.

Now listen to the words of the Antlered God, the Guardian of all things wild and free, Spark of Life yet Keeper of the Gates of Death, whose Call all must answer:

I am the fire within your heart, the yearning of your Soul. I am the Hunter of Knowledge and the Seeker of the Holy Quest; I who stand in the darkness of light; I am He whom you have called Death.

But I am also the seed of life, the joy of existence, the mirth in laughter and the sparkle within thine eyes.

I am the consort, mate, and son of She whom we adore.

Call forth to me with pure intent and love in thine heart, and I shall surely answer.

Heed my call, beloved ones, come unto me and learn the secrets of death and peace. I am the fruit upon the trees and the corn at harvest, He who gives of himself so that others may live.

I am He who leads you home. Scourge and Flame, Blade and Blood, heart and humor, life and death; these are mine and gifts to thee.

Call unto me in the forest wild and on hilltop bare and seek me in the Darkness Bright.

I who have been called Pan, Herne, Osiris, Hades, Cernunnos, Gwyn ap Nudd, and by many other names, speak to thee in thy search. Come dance and sing; come live and smile, for behold: this is my worship.

You are my children and I am thy Father. On swift night wings it is I who lay you at the Mother's feet to be reborn and to return again. I too lie within Her womb, planted in summer seed to live on after my wintry death. For without planting there can be no harvest; without winter there can be no spring; and without death there can be no life.

But thou who thinks to seek me, know that I am the untamed wind, the fury of the storm and the passion within your Soul. Seek me with pride and humility; seek me with strength and tenderness; but seek me best with only love in thine heart.

For this truly is my path, manifest in the endless cycle of birth, death and rebirth as Her great wheel turns the seasons. Celebrate the peak of my power as the midsummer Sun ascends to its zenith; yet hear my call on mid-winter's night and we shall stand together and await the Sun's rebirth.[18]

If working in a group, reading these charges as part of your invocations can be profoundly moving and will definitely serve to intensify the focus of your circle. Reading them out loud can also help in solitary practice, as it allows you to feel a greater connection to both God and Goddess and be secure in the knowledge that they have entered your sacred space to offer their energies for your magickal working. That said, you're not obligated to read these charges. There's absolutely nothing stopping you from writing your own, if you feel so

---

18. Lisa Stewart, *Circle In A Box: Invoking the God/Charge of the Horned God* (New York: Esoteric Productions/Regal Records, 2012).

moved. In fact, we'd wholeheartedly encourage it; we're sure the old gods love to be honored in new ways.

7: Chalice and Blade

This is performed by inserting the athame into the chalice as a representation of the Great Rite, the sacred coupling of God and Goddess from which all life emanates.

Although there are those that differ, within our tradition the male (the person hosting the God) holds the blade, as it represents all things masculine and the energies associated with air and fire. The priestess holds the chalice, as it represents the feminine vessel and the energies of water and earth.

The priestess hands the athame to the priest, signifying her willingness to receive him (it's always on her terms—the God would never force himself upon the Goddess). The priestess offers up the chalice to the priest, saying, "Without him, there could be no darkness." He then raises his athame above the chalice and turns the point down to face the opening of the sacred cup, saying, "Without her, there could be no light." He plunges the blade into the chalice as they both say, "Together, they make this rite complete."

This symbolic act is a form of sympathetic magick, combining their energy and creating fertility or fruitfulness for the ritual or working itself.

When working as a solitary, it is not normal to perform Chalice and Blade by yourself. Instead, we recommend simply laying your athame flat over the cup of the chalice to form a Celtic Cross, a symbol of the union of God and Goddess.

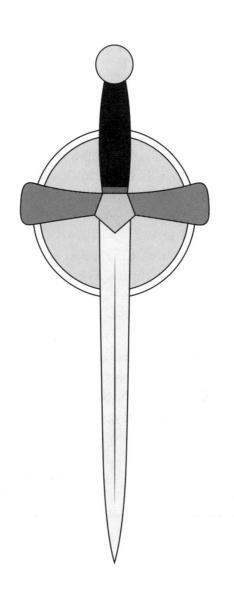

8: The Working Itself: Turning the Wheel or Practical Magick

This is the very reason you cast your circle in the first place, so it is possibly the most important part of the ritual. If you're working in a group, it certainly wouldn't hurt to explain the purpose of the working once again. For example: "Tonight, we will work with the energies of the Cancer full moon, and the focus of the magick is healing."

Hopefully, all within your circle are suitably focused and ready, as now you've brought all the elements, elementals, and the God and Goddess together in your sacred space between the worlds. Their energies are now combined and available to assist in your quest, and the working can begin.

So long as it fits with the intention of the ritual, the world is your oyster. You might do spell work, a meditation or astral journey, perform a group divination or healing, enact a mythic role play, or simply honor your gods in a sabbat rite.

9: Cakes and Ale/Grounding

Although called Cakes and Ale, this step doesn't actually need to have either. You can use whatever food and beverage combination works for you. It could well be small cakes or cookies you've baked yourself, or even fresh fruit and nuts. The ale part could also be water, juice, milk, or even wine, although we would strongly counsel against using any kind of alcoholic beverage when folks will need to drive home from the gathering.

In our tradition, we typically use cakes and ale for grounding. The cakes and ale are blessed with a simple statement: "May we never hunger, may we never thirst, and may we always have enough to share." We often raise considerable energy within the working itself, much like accumulating a static charge. Eating and drinking are great ways of grounding out some excess energy which is returned harmlessly to the earth. Cakes and Ale taken together also allows us to reconnect with our physical bodies. Although this is our usual manner of using cakes and ale for the majority of our rites and rituals, on occasion we use them as a magickal embodiment of the god and goddess by blessing and sharing them just after Chalice and Blade. They are then ingested by the participants before the working itself as added boosts to the magickal energy available.

10 (and 11): Releasing God and Goddess

After the working is complete and before you dismantle your circle, it is time to thank and release your deities.

The order in which they are released is often open to debate, for there are those who feel it should be the reverse of how they were called (last in, first out), and those who feel the God should always be released last and remain in the role of protector until the Goddess has safely departed the rite.

Whatever feels right to you is the way you should go, for even within our own tradition, the priestess representing the Goddess is the one who decides upon who should leave first.

As you speak the words of your devocation with sincere gratitude for the assistance they have given you, feel them leaving the circle and returning whence they came but remaining forever in your heart as part of your magickal family.

12: Releasing the Quarters

Within our tradition we tend to go in reverse order for the majority of our gatherings. That is to say, we begin our releasing in the north and move widdershins (counterclockwise) around the circle to the east. We are always mindful to turn and bow to north at the end, thereby closing the circle and completing the release.

In order to maintain a balanced energy within your rite, the release of each direction should not be too different from the call. And, in the same vein, each release should be largely consistent with the others, varying only in terms of attributes specific to that direction or element.

As before, you can always write your own releases. Again, if you don't know where to start, you can always use those from our gatherings:

Guardians and Elementals of the North,
We give our thanks to thee.
Earth, go now and be free.
Hail, farewell, and blessed be.

Guardians and Elementals of the West,
We give our thanks to thee.
Water, go now and be free.
Hail, farewell, and blessed be.

Guardians and Elementals of the South,
We give our thanks to thee.
Fire, go now and be free.
Hail, farewell, and blessed be.

Guardians and Elementals of the East,
We give our thanks to thee.
Air, go now and be free.
Hail, farewell, and blessed be.

Again, be mindful to close your circle after releasing the last direction, by turning once more to face the north and offering a nod, bow, or other silent recognition.

You may have noticed that we say "blessed be" as opposed to "so mote it be" in our releases. This is because "so mote it be" means "as I speak it, so it is," whereas "blessed be" simply means "may you be blessed," which seems more appropriate for a farewell.

13: Return to the Mundane

This is the act of dissolving the circle. Some call this "opening" and others say "closing," but the idea is exactly the same. You are releasing the space that existed between the worlds back to the mundane and require any nonphysical entities, who gathered and lent their energies to your rite, to go back from whence they came.

In our tradition, the priestess declares: "Let all spirits and elementals attracted to this rite, be on their way now, harming none. Merry meet, merry part, and merry meet again." More often than not, we then sing the traditional circle song by the same name, before yelling "blessed be" rather loudly and clapping a few times to dissipate any excess energy.

As before, you can always use *Circle in a Box* to help release the energies from your circle and return it to the mundane. You can even sing along, if you like. That said, releasing the energy is only part of the process; unless you have the luxury of a dedicated temple or similar space, you must also return the physical space itself back to the mundane, which means properly cleaning and storing your tools, sweeping any ritual salt or other bits and bobs that found their way to the floor during the ritual, and generally tidying up the place so that the only remnant of your magickal working is what's written in your Book of Shadows (which is how it got its name, incidentally).

Some Thoughts on Circle Casting

We've already established that a circle should never be cast without good reason, although casting a circle simply to do a meditation, journey work, or divination is perfectly acceptable. Because we often have magick in mind, here is a little more information on spell working.

Although there are all manners of magickal workings, they basically boil down to just four things: love, prosperity, healing, and spirituality.

From the information we've provided earlier, think about what astrological energies are available to you at the time of your working. Remember to check the moon phase and adjust your spell to work with the energy at hand. If the moon is waxing, it is a great time to build; if it's waning, it is much more suited to releasing.

You may also want to create your spells to work with the energy of the elements. For example, we know from reading through chapter 3 on the elements that earth works well to create stability, so using this elemental energy would be great for a prosperity spell to build a firm foundation and bring in wealth. By the same token, fire is strongly associated with passion, and water with emotion—two great elemental energies for love. The element of air is connected with inspiration and intellect, serving as a great starting point for a spell to awaken spiritual growth.

In determining which elemental energies are available, looking at which sign the moon currently occupies can be of great help:

Air—Aquarius, Gemini, Libra
Fire—Aries, Leo, Sagittarius
Water—Cancer, Scorpio, Pisces
Earth—Taurus, Virgo, Capricorn

By using the elemental energy offered by these signs, we can certainly enhance our work.

A Brief Word about Ethics

By now you are starting to know things. And with knowledge comes power. In fact, some might say that you are beginning to learn things way beyond of the ken of most people. Indeed, great knowledge comes with great power, but with great power also comes great responsibility, for which working magick is no exception. The path of self-gratification at the expense of all others is the path of ruin. In our tradition, we strive to keep pure our highest ideal, and work ever toward it.

We would only perform healing or protection spells on behalf of another with their permission and, even then, we would be mindful to ask that it be for the highest good of all. We would not presume to understand what exactly constitutes the highest good, as we can never see the whole picture. For the same reason, we would never do magick against someone to bring harm or revenge. To do so would mean taking on the role of judge and jury and making a determination of the "facts" based solely upon your personal opinion. You are not a disinterested party and cannot detach yourself from the matter dispassionately. In all likelihood your actions will be shaped by your emotions. Given whatever you put out returns to you threefold, this may not go well, and it will be *you* who suffers.

Summary

In this chapter we've looked at the process of setting up a magickal circle: a place between the worlds, in a time without time. We've looked at the steps involved in casting a circle and the reason we do them. Hopefully, you've learned that whatever happens between the worlds affects all the worlds and as such you must be aware of the consequences of your actions.

If all of this has sunk in, you're now ready to take the next and most important step on the path of the Craft of the Wise: dedication.

nine

The Dedication Rite

This chapter is the culmination of all that has led to this point: your dedication to the old gods. The following pages detail how to prepare for, and perform, a complete dedication ritual to the Lord and Lady.

Preparation for Dedication

Of all the preparations you must make, the first and foremost is that of your mindset: Do you fully understand the nature of the commitment you are about to make, and are you ready to make it?

Dedication is not a trivial act. Have you fully considered the implications of committing yourself to lead a magickal life that honors your deities through your words and deeds?

In a way, this is similar to handfasting in that you are promising yourself (for at the very least a year and a day) to honor and to serve the Craft of the Wise and the family you wish to join.

No matter whether you're making your commitment as part of a group or yours is the personal and private dedication of a solitary practitioner, you should speak your promise out loud, even if your voice shakes.

Write your dedication much like you would create wedding vows, being mindful of not making any promises you are not prepared to keep. It does not matter if you can't offer your deities anything more than your love, for the old gods value simple purity of heart far above failed intentions, no matter how well-meant.

We think it's important that you actually write down the words rather than try and remember what you wanted to say, but wind up forgetting in the emotion of the moment. You could make it rhyme or tell a story; it can be a lengthy speech or a short and sweet promise— whatever feels right to you. Think about your words for a few days prior and feel free to tweak as necessary. Then you can read it during your rite and be able to speak from the heart.

Here is an example of a written dedication:

Great Mother Cerridwen, your hidden child calls to you.

I ask for your love and guidance as I walk upon this path.

In return, I offer you my respect and devotion.

I am at your service, and I will be mindful to help those who walk with me.

I look forward to learning and growing as I work to understand all you have to teach me.

I hear your words, Great Mother; let there be beauty and strength, power and compassion, honor and humility, mirth and reverence within me as I seek to know you. And I know that the seeking and yearning will avail me not, unless I know the Mysteries. I know that which you seek must be found within and I ask you, Great Mother, to guide and guard me on my journey. Blessed be.

What to Wear

If you are dedicating in private, you might choose to work sky-clad, and wear nothing but your birthday suit, other than perhaps a cord with your pouch and athame for easy access.

You might consider wearing a robe that you could make yourself, as there are some pretty simple patterns out there. If sewing is not your thing, you could order a robe from a place you trust. Whichever way you go, do give some thought to the color and material—you are not limited to black velvet.

Above all, being robed or sky-clad is not a requirement; you could wear any clothing you would wear to a special occasion, or even a nice piece of sleepwear. The idea is to make it respectful and comfortable. You probably do not wish to come before the old ones in attire your grandmother would find distasteful.

Where to Hold Your Rite

Some people are lucky enough to have a beautiful and safe outdoor space; if you do, that's wonderful. Wherever you choose, please be sure it is safe from onlookers who might disturb you. Within your home is perfectly acceptable as well.

Be sure to clear the space of anything that might be distracting or seems too mundane. We would also suggest moving out or shutting down any electronic equipment or computer-type things such as cell phones and other devices that might make noise (unless you're using them for backing music).

We would also remind you that your space should be clean and uncluttered. It might be a good idea to tidy up and run the vacuum.

After all, you are inviting some pretty important guests who may not wish to sit on mounds of old newspapers.

Having chosen, secured, and properly prepared your spot, the final step is to choose an appropriate day and time for your ritual. As before, consider the astrological and elemental energies available to you (see chapter 5). Ideally you should plan your dedication to occur on an esbat for a new or full moon. Be sure to record the date in your Book of Shadows or personal journal.

Preparing Yourself: The Ritual Bath

Prior to your dedication, we strongly recommend taking a ritual bath to ensure that you will come to the circle free of unwanted energies, be they negative or simply mundane.

You may wish to place some herbs or oils in the bath water that correspond to the astrological or elemental energies of the day, the deity to whom you are dedicating yourself, or just simply for purification. Whatever you decide to use, just make sure your choices are safe for use and you aren't allergic to any of them.

If you prefer, you could use bath salts instead. You can make your own, or purchase ones that have been made just for this purpose. As a practical tip, we strongly suggest adding oils after you have gotten in, as they tend to sit on the surface of the water and can be irritating to your more delicate parts when sat upon. Herbs might be best contained in some cheese cloth or fillable tea bag so they do not clog the drain.

You might also like to light some special candles or burn some incense to help create a reverent atmosphere and aid your focus. This atmosphere is especially important if you are unable to add anything to your bath perhaps due to allergies. Then it all comes down to intent.

As you sit in the water, be especially mindful of the commitment you are about to make. Feel the water cleansing your pores and pulling away doubt or negative thoughts, especially thoughts about being unworthy or that would in any way hinder you from allowing yourself to move forward.

When you have finished, picture all the unwanted energy, stress, and worry becoming part of the water and leaving as it swirls down the drain. Towel off and proceed to your ritual.

Dedication Ritual

Above all else, this is *your* ritual. Feel free to craft your rite in a way that's just right for you. It can be as elaborate or simple as you want it to be. You could go all-out with a complete altar set using all your tools, or you could simply go out into nature, find a clearing in the forest, and speak from the heart to the ancient ones.

When it comes to the rite itself, there really is no singular "correct" format, but we've included the ritual we use for people dedicating in our own tradition as a starting point. You may use whatever parts you like and add your own personal touches.

Set your altar with something to represent the deities you are inviting, a place for each of the elementals to reside, and any tools you might need such as anointing oil, ritual salt, a water bowl, a candle, incense, and a lighter or matches. Have your athame with you if you have one, but don't worry if you don't; you can simply point your fingers to draw the invoking and banishing pentagrams for each direction.

Invoking and Banishing Pentagrams

Before you begin, you might want to practice drawing the pentagrams shown below until you know them by heart. Start at the point indicated and move in the direction shown by the arrow to trace the pentagram. Remember to overlap the first leg by drawing it again with the final stroke to seal the pentagram.

	Air	Fire	Water	Earth
Invoking				
Banishing				

Now that your preparations are complete, and the allotted hour has come, it's time to begin your ritual.

Approach the altar and stand facing it. Pause and take a deep cleansing breath.

Pick up your salt dish and walk around the border of the circle. You are performing a clearing, so you may go widdershins or deosil, whichever is right for you. If you wish, you can sprinkle a small amount of salt in each of the four corners. However, if you are worried about your pets, hold the bowl and show it to each direction.

Bow or nod as you pause at each quarter. You can work in silence or you may wish to say something like, "With the power of earth, I cleanse and clear my sacred space."

Remember to close your circle after working your way round the quarters, by bowing again to the direction where you started, before returning the salt dish to the altar.

Next, go around the circle with the water bowl in exactly the same way. Again, you may work in silence or say something like, "With the power of water, I cleanse and clear my sacred space." As before, you may sprinkle or just show the water bowl to the direction, depending on your circumstances.

Now purify the circle with the element of fire by going around with the candle. If you're not working in silence, say something like,

"With the power of fire, I cleanse and clear my sacred space." Pause at each quarter and feel the energy of the flame clearing and warming the space. Remember to close your circle by acknowledging the direction in which you started with a bow or nod, before returning the candle to the altar.

Finally, use the incense to represent the element of air, going around once more and, if appropriate, saying, "With the power of air, I cleanse and clear my sacred space." As you work your way around, see any unwanted energy being lifted away in the smoke. As before, seal your circle and return the censer to the altar.

It's not really necessary for you to cleanse and clear yourself with the four elements as you've had a ritual bath and should therefore be clear of any negativity. However, if you feel driven to do so, go right ahead; it certainly can't hurt.

Next, create your sacred space between the worlds by calling the quarters. If working solitary, you can essentially cast your circle simply by calling the quarters. You may begin in the north or east (either is acceptable), but be mindful to close the circle by coming all the way back to where you began or you will have a wedge of space still open. Remember to bow, nod, or otherwise acknowledge the direction in which you started to complete the cast and seal the space.

Assuming you're starting in the east, turn to the direction and say, "All hail to the guardians of the eastern Watchtower. Air, bring forth your elemental power. Great ones of the east, we welcome you. Guard and guide us well. So mote it be." Then draw an air-invoking pentagram with your athame or pointed finger.

Pause for a moment to feel the energies you have summoned arrive.

Now turn to face south and say, "All hail to the guardians of the southern Watchtower. Fire, bring forth your elemental power. Great ones of the south, we welcome you. Guard and guide us well. So mote it be." Now draw a fire-invoking pentagram with your athame or pointed finger.

Pause for a moment to feel the energies you have summoned arrive.

Next, turn to face west and say, "All hail to the guardians of the western Watchtower. Water, bring forth your elemental power. Great ones of the west, we welcome you. Guard and guide us well. So mote it be." Now draw a water-invoking pentagram with your athame or pointed finger.

Pause for a moment to feel the energies you have summoned arrive.

Finally, turn to face north and say, "All hail to the guardians of the northern Watchtower. Earth, bring forth your elemental power. Great ones of the north, we welcome you. Guard and guide us well. So mote it be." Draw an earth-invoking pentagram with your athame or pointed finger.

Pause for a moment to feel the energies you have summoned arrive. When you are done with the north, remember to turn and bow to the east again to complete the circle.

If working alone, you can now come back to the altar and declare the circle cast, saying something like: "I cast and seal this circle in perfect love and perfect trust. Let only love enter and let only love leave. So mote it be." If you're working in a group, you should now proceed to cast the circle hand-to-hand, in the traditional manner (left hand up, right hand down).

With your place between the worlds now created, in a time outside of time, you have now built a suitable space into which to invite your gods.

Invoke your deities by speaking from your heart, ideally out loud. For example, an invocation might be worded as such: "Great Mother Cerridwen, your hidden child calls to you. Come join me for this rite. Come to this space and work your magick. Join me now, Great Mother. So mote it be."

Call to any other energies or witnesses you would like to be present at your dedication: perhaps an ancestor, spirit guide, or guardian.

When you feel all of the energies are present and combined, you can now proceed with your dedication by saying:

> Those who have been called to witness and validate this rite, recognize me, (state your regular name). For I do come before you freely and willingly, without reservation.
>
> I declare, before all those present, that I am prepared to take my oath and work with you.

Now read the dedication you previously prepared, even if your voice shakes.

If we were dedicating a group of people within our tradition, we would now perform a traditional five-fold blessing to welcome each of them to the path. The dedicant's spirit, mouth, heart, hands, and feet are blessed, anointed, and consecrated in turn as the following is read:

> Blessed be thy spirit that remembers the old ways,
> Blessed be thy mouth that speaks the truth,
> Blessed be thy heart that knows the love of the ancient ones,
> Blessed be thy hands that work the magick,
> Blessed be thy feet that walk the path.

If you're working by yourself, you can read this modified version while being conscious of the awakening energies flowing into your physical body:

"Blessed be my spirit that remembers the old ways." Feel energy at the top of your head, the awakening of crown chakra.

"Blessed be my mouth that speaks the truth." Think about how this may relate to you, and how you might express or reveal parts of your journey going forward.

"Blessed be my heart that knows the love of the ancient ones." Feel energy build in your heart center.

"Blessed be my hands that work the magick." Lift your palms upward, and then hold them downward. Feel energy from above and below.

"Blessed be my feet that walk the path." Feel yourself grounded and steadied by the sacred space you are in.

When you're ready, make this statement:

By the power of the goddess Cerridwen, and in front of these witnesses, (if you have called or named any), I now declare myself to be _____ (your magickal name), your hidden child and dedicant for one year and one day. By your grace, may I grow and learn as I walk on this path filled with mystery.

Although this concludes your personal dedication, you're still standing in a circle that contains some serious magickal energy. Rather than just close, you might want to avail yourself of its energy. For example, you could meditate or do a small bit of divination for yourself, perhaps pulling a card for inspiration or empowering a crystal to carry with you for this turn of the Wheel.

When you are ready, it's time to thank and release those whom you have called. Release any witnesses, guardians, or guides you asked to join the rite using your own words. Then release your deities by saying something like, "Great Mother Cerridwen, I do thank you for witnessing this rite and guiding me well. I release you from this space but ask that you remain forever in my heart. Go in peace. Go in love. Blessed be."

Now begin the process of returning to your place between the worlds back to the mundane by releasing the quarters. Again, you may choose to release them deosil or widdershins, whichever feels right to you.

Assuming you are releasing widdershins, start in the north. Turn to face the direction and say:

> Guardians and elementals of the north, I do give my thanks to thee. Earth, I release you now. Go forth and be free. Hail, farewell, and blessed be.

Draw an earth-banishing pentagram and visualize the elemental energy being released and moving out of the circle. Bow before turning to the next direction.

Now turn to face west and say:

> Guardians and elementals of the west, I do give my thanks to thee. Water, I release you now. Go forth and be free. Hail, farewell, and blessed be.

Draw a water-banishing pentagram and visualize the elemental energy being released and moving out of the circle. Bow before turning to the next direction.

Now turn to face south and say:

Guardians and elementals of the south, I do give my
thanks to thee. Fire, I release you now. Go forth and be
free. Hail, farewell, and blessed be.

Draw a fire-banishing pentagram and visualize the elemental
energy being released and moving out of the circle. Bow before turning to the next direction.

Finally turn to face east and say:

Guardians and elementals of the east, I do give my thanks
to thee. Air, I release you now. Go forth and be free. Hail,
farewell, and blessed be.

Draw an air-banishing pentagram and visualize the elemental
energy being released and moving out of the circle. Bow as before.

In the same way as when you were calling the quarters, remember
to close your ring by turning once more to the north and acknowledge the direction with a bow or nod to finish the release.

Conclude the rite by returning to the altar and saying:

The old gods have been well served and my dedication
witnessed. I declare this circle open but unbroken. Let
all spirits and elementals attracted to this rite be on their
way now, harming none. Merry meet, merry part, and
merry meet again. Blessed be.

Congratulations, you have completed your dedication rite. All
that remains is to return the space itself back to the mundane by putting everything away properly and tidying up. Remember your duty

of care for your magickal tools. Don't just toss them in a drawer—clean them and store them in their proper place.

We would also strongly recommend that you make a record in your personal Book of Shadows or weirdness journal while the events of your ritual are still fresh in your mind.

ten

Where Do We Go from Here?

This chapter speaks about leading a magickal life—being able to transcend the profane and walk in beauty. We explore how your actions, deeds, words, and even thoughts can serve to honor the Divine and inspire others. We look at ways in which you can keep yourself inspired and motivated to continue your spiritual growth. And we consider some practical steps you can take to maintain both your own progress along the path of the Craft of the Wise, as well as how to tend to the path itself so it will remain available to whomever follows in your footsteps.

The Journey Onward

In making your dedication, you have reached a very important juncture on the path of the Craft of the Wise, but it is far from the end of your journey. In fact, some would say it's just the beginning. Certainly, you're in a very different place than when you made your first tentative steps upon this well-worn path, but there is still a long road ahead of you that's full of amazing and rewarding experiences.

Although there isn't space to explore the fascinating subject of numerology here, you'll find that the number three is notably signifi-cant and pops up quite frequently within the world of Witchery. Your journey onward serves as a case in point—it basically comes down to three things: your individual spiritual development, your responsibil-ity to honor the Craft and deities through words and deeds, and your duty to support others on this path as well as the preservation of the path itself so it remains available for all to follow.

Personal Spiritual Development

There is an old piece of Zen wisdom that states, "That which you are seeking is causing you to seek."

While there is always a sense of achievement whenever folks complete one of the training courses within our tradition, it's our experience that they often experience a form of separation anxiety and can't wait to sign up for the next course. Having made it through this book, it's more than likely that you've opened the door that has no key and acquired a taste for learning and an appetite for knowl-edge. So, what's next? Where do you go from here? Well, the good news is you have options … lots of them! What's more, you can pur-sue more than one at a time.

One of the first things we would suggest is to read a few books. Go for quality rather than quantity, and choose books written by or about respected Craft elders. We touched on the history of the Craft in the first chapter, but there is much more you can and probably should learn, too.

Perhaps the best place to start (like we did in this book) is with the two people who helped make the Craft what it is today—Gerald

Gardner and Doreen Valiente. If you are looking for the most accurate accounts, you should go directly to the source and get it from the horse's mouth, so to speak. To that end we strongly suggest that you read all the books they've written that you can lay your hands on, especially *Witchcraft Today* by Gerald Gardner (originally published 1954) and *Where Witchcraft Lives* by Doreen Valiente (originally published 1962). We would also highly recommend their "official" biographies written by Philip Heselton, *Wiccan Roots: Gerald Gardner and the Modern Witchcraft Revival* (published 2000) and *Doreen Valiente: Witch* (published 2016).

In addition to broadening your knowledge by reading, you might also want to learn a divinatory skill, as it can definitely help deepen your connection to spirit while developing your intuition. As before, you have lots of options—there is a "-mancy" for just about anything you can think of. Consider what speaks to you (pun intended) and practice. Even if you're not a naturally gifted psychic and your intuition presents a challenge to develop, the very act of working to cultivate a divinatory skill will teach you the art of observation, which is key to understanding the nature of nature itself.

Although the choice of divinatory skill is entirely up to you, we would suggest spending at least some time with one in particular: the tarot. Tarot is a great tool not only for divination, but also for meditation and spell work. If you don't yet have a deck, we strongly suggest that you start with the original Rider-Waite-Smith tarot, upon which almost every modern tarot deck is based, as the cards hold much wisdom hidden in plain sight. Even the word used to describe the cards in the deck, *arcana*, shares the root for the word "arcane," meaning mysterious or secret, understood by few.

Aside from digging into the history of the Craft and honing your divinatory skills, you can also aid your personal growth by delving into the subjects/pursuits listed here:

- Herbalism: A tool for healing or for incense-making.

- Astrology: A discipline for planetary insight, understanding the Wheel of the Year and the cycles of the moon, and magickal timing.

- Meditation: A practice that serves as a way to become closer to the gods, self-exploration, and/or to perfect your journey work.

- Kitchen Witchery and Hearth Magick: These disciplines help you fully live a magickal life. You'll be able to keep in step with your body and home and be mindful of the Earth and all its inhabitants.

- Healing (for yourself and others): This practice has obvious benefits. Perhaps take a hands-on healing course, like Reiki or chakra crystal healing.

- Find out more about crystals and their offerings.

- Experiment and practice spell working and keep a log of what works and what doesn't.

- Build an even stronger relationship with your gods. Learn all you can about them.

It's also very important to continue to progress along the well-worn path with your spiritual practices. While you are certainly free to remain a solitary practitioner, you may want to find out about groups in your area and check them out to see if they're a good fit energetically. Just be mindful that some groups/traditions are more open and welcoming than others and that not all groups fit all people, and vice versa.

There are many Wiccan traditions and Witchcraft practices in existence today. Do your research and hunt around for one that speaks to you. When you've found something that resonates with you, do like Doreen Valiente did all those years ago—get in touch. Rest assured that if you're coming from a place of sincerity, the people won't be offended.

If there are no suitable local groups, you might also consider forming one of your own. That's not to say that you should declare yourself High Priest/Priestess and attempt to form your own tradition at this stage. Setting up a study group with a couple of like-minded individuals can really help you all learn and grow together.

Honoring the Craft

We've touched on the subject of ethics in a couple of places, but now that you've taken the step of dedication to your gods, ethics will assume far greater importance. You must continually strive to ensure that your thoughts, words, and deeds honor both your deities and the Craft of the Wise itself. However, this is nowhere near the heavy burden it seems like if your head is in the right place. You just have to remember that energy follows thought. Be mindful that your thoughts become your words, and your words become your actions, so you may need to rethink your thinking.

It may sound obvious, but whatever you focus upon becomes the object of your focus and its energies are emphasized and enhanced. If you're focused on what's wrong, you'll quickly notice that there's something wrong with most everything you look at. This in turn only serves to reinforce your negative focus; it actually feeds upon itself and your day goes from bad to worse. On the other hand, if you consciously change your focus to what's right, you will instead start to appreciate the wonderful things that surround you with a renewed sense of gratitude.

When we humans make the transition from spirit to become incarnate in our physical bodies, our perspective becomes brutally curtailed as we become the center of our own universe and the sole frame of reference for our reality. Again, we see from where we're standing. While it's easy to see how things affect us, when we walk the path of the Craft of the Wise, we need to be mindful of how we affect things.

It is important to make a conscious and concerted effort to attune to your higher self and endeavor to take the high road whenever possible. Conduct yourself with pride, but remember to be humble. Be gracious and tolerant of others; do not allow their actions to frustrate you. Chances are that they're not even directed at you anyway; you're seeing things from your point of view, which is unlikely to be completely unbiased. Certainly, someone else may have a story you don't know and may well be dealing with their own unique set of problems; don't allow them to become yours. Instead, work to spread joy and happiness wherever you can. Practice random acts of kindness: hold a door for someone, pick up something that's been dropped, offer your seat to someone who needs it more on a bus or train, and above all, simply smile and say good morning/afternoon/evening to people you meet on the street, at the post office, or in the grocery store.

Be mindful also to honor your deities by practicing respect for all living things, including Mother Earth herself. And while it certainly is laudable to support environmental causes, try to remember that it's the little things that make the biggest differences. Be aware of your own environmental impact and carbon footprint. Reduce, reuse, and recycle. If you don't absolutely need to take the car, walk instead. Don't litter … or better yet, pick up that discarded wrapper, bottle, or can and dispose of it properly. While it's true that a single person may not be able to change the world, you can bring a world of change to place where you live.

Supporting Others and the Path Itself

Every journey has a beginning, even if it has no end. Although we may walk the path until the day we shuffle off this mortal coil to join our ancestors, each of us began our journey by taking our first tentative step onto this well-worn path. By doing so, we have each become indebted to those who have gone before. Remember that if it were not for the efforts of our forebears to preserve the path, it may well have been lost in the sands of time.

It's certainly true that the champions of modern Wicca, Gerald Gardner and Doreen Valiente, did much to ensure the survival of the Craft, but they were far from the only ones. In fact, we owe those who came after them an immense debt of gratitude, for without those authors, poets, priests, and priestesses who dedicated themselves to guiding others along the path, it may have fallen into disrepair through neglect and been unavailable for anyone to follow.

In dedicating yourself to the Craft, you too are accepting the responsibility to assist those behind you when and wherever you can. If someone should express an interest in learning more, suggest some of the resources or books you found most helpful—or even lend them one if you are able.

One of the most effective ways of ensuring that the path will always be available to those who would follow in your footsteps is by supporting those organizations that work to support it. Although there are a number of such organizations, one we feel particularly worthy of support is the Doreen Valiente Foundation, a UK-based charitable trust dedicated to preserving the legacy of one the most influential people in the history of modern Witchcraft (as you recall from the first chapter). The foundation was established in 2011 by Doreen's last High Priest, John Belham-Payne, to protect her collection of magickal tools and artifacts from being sold off (as happened to those left behind by Gerald Gardner), and perhaps more importantly, to ensure that the sizable bequest of her profoundly moving poems remains available to the Craft. It is with the kind permission of the Doreen Valiente Foundation that we are able to include the quotations from the Charge of the Goddess that appear within this book and thereby introduce you to her incredible work.

You can learn more about the foundation and the important work they do by visiting their website. While there, we would urge you to consider making a donation no matter how small, or even becoming a member yourself.[19] It really is a practical way of maintaining the well-worn path in order that it continues to be available for others.

In closing, we'd like to congratulate you for having the dedication to stay the course to the end of this book. We sincerely hope it has been useful to you on your journey and given you a good foundation into the religion of modern Wicca. Perhaps it's even provided an understanding of some things you didn't know you didn't know.

As you journey onward from this point, you will certainly face many challenges. But if you take the wisdom of Doreen Valiente to heart and keep pure your highest ideal by striving ever toward it, you will be just fine.

Journey well!

---

19. The official website of The Doreen Valiente Foundation, http://www .doreenvaliente.org (last accessed May 14, 2019).

Bibliography/ Suggested Further Reading

Bracelin, Jack. *Gerald Gardner: Witch*. London: Octagon Press, 1960.

Gardner, Gerald B. *Witchcraft Today*. New York: Citadel Press, 2004. Originally published 1954 by Rider & Co.

Gardner, Gerald B., writing as Scire. *High Magic's Aid*. Clevedon, UK: Aurinia Books, 2010. Originally published 1949 by Houghton.

Harris, Amy L., and Virginia J. Vitzhum. "Darwin's Legacy: An Evolutionary View of Women's Reproductive and Sexual Functioning." *The Journal of Sex Research*, vol. 50. Abingdon, UK: Routledge, 2013.

Heselton, Philip. *Doreen Valiente: Witch*. Brighton, UK: The Doreen Valiente Foundation, 2016.

Heselton, Philip. *Gerald Gardner and the Cauldron of Inspiration: An Investigation into the Sources of Gardnerian Witchcraft.* Taunton, UK: Capall Bann, 2000.

———. *Wiccan Roots.* Taunton, UK: Capall Bann, 2000.

Lieber, Arnold J. and Jerome Agel. *The Lunar Effect: Biological Tides and Human Emotions.* New York: Dell Publishing, 1980.

Murray, Margaret A. *The God of the Witches.* New York: Oxford University Press, 1970.

Rogers, Nicholas. *Halloween: From Pagan Ritual to Party Night.* New York: Oxford University Press, 2002.

Simms, Maria Kay. *The Witch's Circle: Rituals and Craft of the Cosmic Muse.* St. Paul, MN: Llewellyn Worldwide, 1996.

Stewart, Lisa. *Circle in a Box* (CD recording). New York: Esoteric Productions/Regal Records, 2012.

Valiente, Doreen. *The Charge of the Goddess: The Poetry of Doreen Valiente.* Brighton, UK: The Doreen Valiente Foundation, 2014.

Wohlleben, Peter. *The Hidden Life of Trees: What They Feel, How They Communicate.* Berkeley, CA: Greystone Books, 2016.

Glossary

Alban Arthan: *See* Yule.

Alban Eilir: *See* Ostara.

Alban Elfed: *See* Mabon.

Alban Hefin: *See* Litha.

Anoint: To dab, smear, or rub with oil, wine, or any other substance as part of a consecration rite or ritual.

Asperge: To ceremonially sprinkle with saltwater as part of a consecration rite or ritual.

Athame: A sacred blade used to channel and direct energy.

Banish: To dismiss or send away the energies, qualities, or persona of divine (or elemental) origin from oneself, a group, or sacred space. The opposite of invocation.

Beltane: One of the eight Wiccan observances that honor the Wheel of the Year, this greater (terrestrial) sabbat celebrates the beginning of summer and is typically held on or about May 1.

Calan Haf: Also called Calan Mai. *See* Beltane.

Calan Gaeaf: *See* Samhain.

Calan Mai: Also called Calan Haf. *See* Beltane.

Cense: To ceremonially perfume with burning incense as part of a consecration rite or ritual.

Consecrate: To make sacred by means of ritually anointing, asperging, or censing an object or person.

Cowan: This is the word used within the Craft to describe persons unknowledgeable of or uninitiated into the arts magickal—those Harry Potter and his kind would call muggles.

Cross-Quarters: The points on the Wheel of the Year, exactly midway between the lesser (solar) sabbats, where some Wiccan groups hold the greater (terrestrial) sabbats. Typically, this is on or about the seventh day of the month in which the sabbat is held.

Deosil: The direction with or in accordance to the movement of the sun. This is clockwise in the Northern Hemisphere and counterclockwise in the Southern Hemisphere.

Deva: A plant deva is the spirit or etheric body of the plant. The word comes from Sanskrit and means "divine being" or "god."

Ecliptic: This is the "great circle," the path the sun appears to follow on the earth's surface as the earth proceeds on its year-long journey around the sun. It is so called as the only time solar or lunar eclipses can occur is when the moon crosses this path.

Ephemeris: An ephemeris is a collection of tables that list the zodiacal position of the astral bodies in relation to the earth for given dates and times. Originally published in printed form, they are now more commonly included as part of astrological computer programs and can often be accessed online. Nonetheless, a few ephemerides (the plural of ephemeris) are still available in book form and are well worth a look if you can get your hands on one.

Esbat: Wiccan rite or ritual held to honor a specific phase of the moon. Most commonly the full moon, but new moon, first quarter, and last quarter may also be celebrated.

Geocentric: Literally "'Earth at the center." A term most often used to describe the practice of traditional astrology, which looks at the perceived movement of the sun, moon, and planets in relation to the fixed stars as viewed from Earth.

Grounding: The action of dissipating excess energy raised during rites, rituals, or magickal workings harmlessly into the earth.

Gwyl Awst: *See* Lughnasadh.

Gwyl Ffraid: *See* Imbolc.

Imbolc: One of the eight Wiccan observances that honors the Wheel of the Year. This greater (terrestrial) sabbat celebrates the beginning of spring and is typically held on or about February 2.

Invoke: To summon or call the energies, qualities, or persona, of divine (or elemental) origin into oneself, a group, or sacred space. The opposite of banishment. Not to be confused with "evoke" (or its root word, "evocative," which means "to create or stimulate feelings, emotions, or memories").

Litha: One of the eight Wiccan observances that honors the Wheel of the Year, this lesser (solar) sabbat corresponds to the summer solstice and is typically held on or about June 21.

Lughnasadh: One of the eight Wiccan observances that honors the Wheel of the Year, this greater (terrestrial) sabbat celebrates the beginning of autumn and is typically held on or about August 1.

Mabon: One of the eight Wiccan observances that honors the Wheel of the Year, this lesser (solar) sabbat corresponds to the autumnal equinox and is typically held on or about September 21. Pedantic pronunciation pointer: Say "mab" as in "blab," not "mabe" as in "babe."

Ostara: One of the eight Wiccan observances that honors the Wheel of the Year, this lesser (solar) sabbat corresponds to the spring equinox and is typically held on or about March 21.

Pantheon: A word used to describe all the gods, goddesses, and other deities of a people or religion, seen as a whole or a family.

Pentacle: A pentagram enclosed by a circle. May also refer to jewelry depicting this symbol.

Pentagram: Ancient sacred symbol of a five-pointed star, whose points represent the four elements of earth, air, fire, and water, together with spirit.

Power hand: Your projective or dominant hand, used to wield magickal tools or draw magickal symbols such as invoking and banishing pentagrams. Typically, the hand with which you write.

Sabbat: A Wiccan rite or ritual to honor a specific point in the Wheel of the Year.

Samhain: One of the eight Wiccan observances that honors the Wheel of the Year, this greater (terrestrial) sabbat celebrates the beginning of winter and is typically held on or about October 31.

Synodic period: The time taken to return to the starting point in a lunar cycle (i.e., the period between one full moon and the next). From the Greek *synod,* a word meaning "meeting," "assembly," or "coming together." The synodic period of the moon (29.53 days) is longer than the time it takes to actually orbit the earth (27.32 days), as the earth is itself orbiting the sun, thereby affecting the moon's aspect to it.

Wand: A magickal tool, typically made of wood, used to channel and direct energy.

Widdershins: The direction against or in opposition to the movement of the sun. This is counterclockwise in the northern hemisphere and clockwise in the southern hemisphere.

Ysbrydnos: A Welsh word meaning "night of spirits," where the veils between the worlds are at their thinnest. These occur at the liminal times of the year, Calan Gaeaf (Samhain) and Calan Haf (Beltane).

Yule: One of the eight Wiccan observances that honors the Wheel of the Year, this lesser (solar) sabbat corresponds to the winter solstice and is typically held on or about December 21.

Zodiac: The collection of twelve astrological signs from Aries to Pisces. Literally, "circle of animals," although, strictly speaking, the sign and constellation of Libra is not an animal, but a set of scales.

To Write to the Authors

If you wish to contact the authors or would like more information about this book, please write to the authors in care of Llewellyn Worldwide Ltd. and we will forward your request. Both the authors and publisher appreciate hearing from you and learning of your enjoyment of this book and how it has helped you. Llewellyn Worldwide Ltd. cannot guarantee that every letter written to the authors can be answered, but all will be forwarded. Please write to:

Lisa & Anton Stewart
℅ Llewellyn Worldwide
2143 Wooddale Drive
Woodbury, MN 55125-2989

Please enclose a self-addressed stamped envelope for reply,
or $1.00 to cover costs. If outside the U.S.A., enclose
an international postal reply coupon.

Many of Llewellyn's authors have websites with additional information and resources. For more information, please visit our website at http://www.llewellyn.com